ORIENTALISM
&
HISTORY

ORIENTALISM

&

HISTORY

EDITED BY

Denis Sinor

SECOND EDITION

Indiana University Press

Bloomington & London

To the memory of
HENRI FRANKFORT
this book is dedicated
by his
fellow contributors.

BERNARD LEWIS
J. E. VAN LOHUIZEN - DE LEEUW
EDWIN G. PULLEYBLANK
DENIS SINOR

CONTENTS

PREFACE

THE study of the past was not always so general as its present popularity in Europe would suggest. As a rule, non-European historians dealt only with the past of their own community, their curiosity not going beyond the break that separated the historical continuity in which they lived from that which preceded it. No hard and fast rules can be laid down as to what criteria have determined each of these continuities, what combination of social, linguistic or religious factors distinguishes one historical entity from another.

European civilisation is, perhaps, the oldest still extant historical continuity, for it is not only the direct linear descendant of Greek civilisation, but—at least through Christendom if not also through other channels—it is the heir to the civilisation of the Ancient Near East. It is no. doubt this mixed character of their own civilisation that has helped the European historians to a broader outlook on the human past and a better understanding of it than has been shown by historians belonging to other civilisations.

If this outlook is not limited to Europe in the geographical sense, it still remains narrow; only the history of the Ancient Near East has so far been universally acknowledged as a study worth undertaking for itself. Perhaps such studies are felt to be "justified" by the spiritual indebtedness of our own civilisation to the Ancient Near East. For other extra-European studies interest remains still very limited. Although in recent years much progress has been made in ensuring oriental studies the place they deserve, they have failed so far to obtain full recognition. It is always difficult to convince people that what they do not know can be as important as what they know. Under the pressure of events the importance of Asia's present is more and more being recognised, but its past is still very far from receiving the consideration it deserves. A handful of orientalists are endeavouring to tackle a task infinitely greater in scope than the sum of what could be called European studies, which are served by so many scholars.

ix

Which specialist of the Venetian school of painting would be expected to be also an expert in Italian economy, let alone in the French revolution or in Shakespearian studies? Yet similar exigencies are not uncommon when it comes to oriental studies. A historian of China may be expected to have expert knowledge not only of the whole history of China, but also of its art, literature and religions, and will often be consulted also on things Japanese or Indo-Chinese. With such demands upon him it is small wonder that, much of the time, he is unable to attain the high standard of scholarship expected in European studies.

It would be unjust on this account to pass harsh judgment upon what has been done in oriental studies. Indeed, if we consider the width of the field, the achievements of the scholars labouring in it must command respect. It is only regrettable that the results of their research, admirable though they often are, tend to be hidden away in periodicals of small circulation, and to remain unknown beyond the narrow circle of specialists. With some commendable exceptions, such as, generally speaking, the history of the Ancient Near East, more general publications known to and used by wider circles are either out of date or unreliable, or both. It can be said that at present, in the field of oriental history, the data made available by the orientalist to the non-specialist constitute but a fraction of what is in fact known on the subject. Even worse, the non-specialist very often neither has a clear picture of the difficulties he has to overcome to attain knowledge, nor knows the limitations inherent in orientalist research.

The principal aim of this book is to bring, as far as historical studies are concerned, some relief to this deficiency. We have sought to contribute to a better integration of oriental history with general history. To achieve this end we have found it desirable to indicate to the general historian some of the problems particular to oriental researches, and to suggest to orientalists perhaps a fuller realisation of how their fields of study can, and should, be set at their proper place in general history. The plan, in itself, is ambitious; but, as I have said, we have sought only to contribute to the solution of the problem, none of us thinking to have solved it.

As the Orient includes, in fact, almost everything that is not Western in tradition, the first necessary step in writing this book seemed to be its disintegration into organic units, its division into areas. This division turned out to be a fairly easy task, and each region—the word is not to be taken in its geographical sense—was given a separate chapter. Few will debate, we hope, the justification of the division adopted, although some may deplore that the division has not been carried further. Egypt or Mesopotamia, China or Japan, to give only two examples, might have been treated in separate chapters. We did not think it desirable, however, to divide our chapters in small units, and it is to be hoped that in going through the book, the reader will adopt our point of view. I regret only the absence of a chapter on pre-Islamic Iran. The lack of sufficient material, together with the relatively short span of time that such a chapter would have covered, made me abandon the idea of seeking the collaboration of yet another specialist, preliminary talks with experts having suggested that pre-Islamic Iran could not have figured as a partner of equal rights with the other areas treated in this book.

The five chapters which compose the present book follow, broadly speaking, the same pattern; a definition in space and time of the area with which each is concerned, a survey of its main characteristics, and an outline of its principal achievements. We have also endeavoured to call attention to the influence each area has exerted on the rest of the world. The second part of each chapter deals with literary and other sources relative to the area, with particular reference to difficulties inherent to their study. We have not sought to give "history in a nutshell," nor to produce an elementary guidebook, but have hoped that our personal assessment and interpretation of five civilisations and of the studies related to them, however short, might give food for thought to the specialist as well as to the general historian.

The idea that such a book should be written sprang up somewhat belatedly, in January 1954, in connexion with the preparations for the 23rd International Congress of Orientalists. It was felt that at this occasion it might be opportune to recall that, manifold as oriental studies may be, the interest in the historical is common to them all.

I am very grateful to my co-authors for undertaking to write their share without previous notice and in less than three months; Professor Lewis had even to produce his paper while engaged in a lecture-tour in the U.S.A. One of us did not live to see the publication of our book. The sad news of H. Frankfort's death reached me a few hours after I had dispatched to him the page-proofs of his chapter, accompanied by congratulations on his recent election as a Fellow of the British Academy.

My thanks are due to Messrs. Heffer and Sons for undertaking to publish and print this book at such short notice.

D. S.

Cambridge, 26th July. 1954.

PREFACE TO THE SECOND EDITION

THE first edition of *Orientalism and History* has been out of print for many years. Originally the book was conceived of as a sort of working paper, a basis for further discussions which were to take place at a meeting devoted to "Orientalism and History" during the 23rd International Congress of Orientalists held in Cambridge in August 1954. After so many years I can unabashedly admit that I intended to use my position as Secretary-General of that congress to make at least some of the participants aware of the magnitude of the problems involved in the writing of Asian history and of the means and methods employed to solve them.

Subsequently a more ambitious project was carried out by Professor C. H. Philips, Director of the School of Oriental and African Studies, University of London, who had been chairman of the "Orientalism and History" meeting of the Congress. Between 1956 and 1958, he convened a number of study conferences "to survey and evaluate the course and character of historical writing on the peoples of Asia." The papers read at these conferences were later published under the general title *Historical writing on the peoples of Asia*.[1] Valuable as they are, most of the papers contained in these volumes were written for the expert rather than for the general reader; they deal more with the trees than the forest. I feel, therefore, that they do not in any way preclude the usefulness of a second edition of *Orientalism and History*, and I have been encouraged in this feeling by the kind reception given to the first edition and by the steadily growing interest in Asian history.

Had the contributors of this volume been faced with the task of rewriting their respective essays, they might have done them differently. None of us, however, felt the urge to disavow the ideas expressed a little over fifteen years ago. Consequently, the essays are published in their original form, but with the bibliographical notes expanded and brought up to date. Henri Frankfort's contribution, a modest monument to the memory of this great scholar, stands unaltered, frozen as it were by his untimely death.

The willingness of the original contributors to write new bibliographical notes seems to indicate that all those who worked on the first edition kept a soft spot in their hearts for this little volume. I am deeply appreciative of their continued interest and of their additional efforts for the preparation of the present edition.

*   *   *

It is often stated that the concept "Asia" is geographical rather than historical, imposed from outside and unknown to the inhabitants of that great continent. While this may be so, it in no way impairs the validity of the term. The bat, the elephant, and the whale, different as they are, are all mammals, even though they are unaware of this fact. A divisional concept does not lose its validity because the entities to which it is applied are unaware of its existence. Thus, notwithstanding its Western origin, the term "Asia" is a perfectly valid one. The Epilogue of this book will show that definitions *per genus et differentiam* can be used to make distinctions among various parts of Asia. Why should we recoil from applying them to the correlative concepts of Europe and Asia? Orientalism is that branch of scholarship which uses Western methods to elucidate problems pertaining to lands lying east of the European ecumene, and this book examines the several aspects of Western historiography concerned with these problems.

The question is not so much whether a valid distinction can be made between European and Asian history, but whether scholars representing the intellectual tradition of Europe are willing and able to write world history, with Western methods to be sure, but without the Western provincialism that mars all too many of the supposedly objective studies of social scientists. Mankind shares few universals, even where physical, countable elements are involved. The endurance of the human body is far from being the same in different epochs and among different races and it is certainly not in proportion—as Western medical science tends to assume—to the calories or vitamins absorbed by the individual. There is no physiological explanation for a wiry Turkish *hamal*'s being able to carry weights under which a better fed and actually stronger Western porter would collapse. That man must eat to live is certainly a statement of universal validity, but to venture much beyond such a truism and establish the food required daily by "man" is a very risky undertaking. When we enter the domain of the spiritual, the difficulty of establishing universals increases.

The historian must remember that the notions and activities of any individual are meaningful only if set against their own background. The description of a seemingly simple event may be misleading when, in distinguishing the important from the trivial, it fails to take into account the standards of those taking part in the event. By way of illustration one may cite the example of Mongol historical sources which attach far less importance to the conquests of Chingis Khan than to what seem to us the rather petty internal skirmishes between various Mongol factions. While we may question the judgment of the Mongol historian contemporary with Chingis, it would be a serious mistake to ignore his scale of values, which may be most revealing on the inner springs of Mongol history.

The historian's task is to reconstruct, understand, explain, and narrate the past in terms understandable to his reader but not in the light of his own standards. How high the degree of incomprehension can be is apparent even among Western historians dealing with components of their own world which are other than those in which they are rooted. The dismay with which men of Germanic—Anglo-Saxon orientation normally view those representing a Latin heritage is a good case in point, but incomprehension reaches tragic proportions in the confrontation of the Western tradition with the civilizations of Asia. This lack of comprehension can no longer be ascribed to a lack of interest. It is the result, I submit, of an intellectual laziness which engenders the mistaken belief that the recent period of Western impact, which has been relatively short, is of decisive importance in the history of Asia. An unduly high percentage of Western works focuses on this short period of dominant Western influence and is, in fact, quite often nothing other than the history of Western man in Asia. As Professor

Georg Morgenstierne put it, "The horizon of Western historians has till recently often been circumscribed by national
and occidental hedges. Too often the Orient was only a stage
where the Asiatic mute actors just passed through while the
heroic parts were played by Europeans."[2]

I do not wish to deny the importance of the Western impact
on Asia, but I think it is high time to view it in its proper
perspective. Closer scrutiny will reveal that, in essence, it is
limited to technology; transport, telecommunications, and industrial and medical techniques, not to mention devices even
more useful such as guns, bombs, tanks, and the atom bomb,
all of them brain-children of Western civilization and all of
them in great demand, have either been adopted or have been
accepted as worthy of adoption by virtually the whole world.
More significant and less recent are the adoption of the
Western calendar and of the very idea that even small fractions
of time are worth measuring. This latter habit—a result of the
multiplication of cheap and handy time-pieces—has not yet
penetrated very deeply in the lower strata of Asian societies
whose sense of time remains very different from that of the
Western man. The extent of foreign influence should not be
measured by its effect on only one section of the society, such
as the governing class, but rather by the depth of its penetration through all classes of the society. Much importance
should be, and seldom is, attached to the spread of Western
hair styles for men, Western foot-wear, and some Western
eating habits. However, knife and fork have failed to oust
chopsticks (or fingers for that matter), and the Western staple
food, bread made with yeast, has never gained widespread
popularity in Asia. The use of rice and tea by the West has
not been paralleled in Asia by the adoption on a similar scale
of any Western food.

One must agree with John K. Fairbank's words that "the
peoples of East Asia have been highly selective in their borrowings from the West, clinging to those patterns within their
ancient and mature cultures that are not definitely inconsistent
with the modernizing trend. Only some among the Western
techniques, institutions, and ideas produced an impact on them
and were borrowed out of fear or admiration. Others were

despised or ignored."³ Closer scrutiny would reveal that most of the Western techniques borrowed are directly or indirectly pertinent to war, and that techniques not closely connected with military interests—for example, those used in agriculture—have had, relatively speaking, little effect.

However important, technology is but one part of any civilization, and in all other fields the West has had an astonishingly small impact on Asia. Western art in its infinite varieties and many branches, from architecture through painting to music, has failed to make serious inroads in Asia where, after almost two thousand years, Christian influence remains minimal. Western political systems have openly or *de facto* been rejected almost everywhere. Even where they have been formally adopted, usually under Western military pressure, their application is such as to change their original functions. This is not only true for the parliamentary system or for Western-type democracy, but also for Marxism, which, outside the Soviet Union and in so far as its intellectual concept is concerned, has failed in Asia.

Taken in historical perspective, effective Western rule over parts of Asia has been short-lived and relatively superficial. Its study is certainly justified but it hardly deserves the almost exclusive attention it often receives. One cannot help suspecting that this predilection may be due not only to Western provincialism but also to the fact that the modern relevant sources in Western languages can be handled more easily than the pre-Western materials in their original languages.

Historiography is one of those fields of intellectual endeavour which might be benefited by an increase of Western influence on Asian minds. The superiority of the Western method of historical research over, for example, its Muslim or Chinese counterparts—however venerable their traditions may be—can hardly be denied. Speaking of Muslim India, Professor Aziz Ahmad remarked: "Within the various disciplines of Western scholarship the one Muslim Indian intellectuals found simultaneously most fascinating and most challenging was the Western orientalist approach to Islamic history. . . . Western orientalists with their sound linguistic scholarship, their first-hand knowledge of primary Arabic sources, and their effort at objectivity . . . posed for the Indian Muslim intellectual a . . . difficult problem of challenge and response."[4] The number of Asian scholars using these Western methods is still small, and, not unnaturally, the results of their efforts continue to have more in common with the nationalist historians of the nineteenth century—Macaulay, Michelet, Treitschke, or Bancroft— than with the critical historical scholarship whose origins we usually associate with the name of Ranke. Complete historical objectivity can never be achieved, but historiography can and should liberate itself from the contingencies of short-term political aims. For the time being, Western historians, particularly in their dealing with the periods prior to that of greater Western influence, are more immune to this danger than their Asian colleagues. It may be assumed that the latter have a deeper and more accurate understanding of their own civilization's mentality than do Western historians. When this understanding is not used for apologetic or political purposes it may even add a new dimension to our knowledge. However, for many years to come the need for Western historians to focus their attention on Asia will remain, and they will continue to face a double task. Like all historians, they must shed light on the past, but they must also provide the Western reader with an insight into civilizations other than his own. The understanding thus brought about, although not political in motivation, but simply the by-product of an attempt to increase our knowledge, may have a beneficial effect upon international relations.

Bloomington, 1969   D. S.

Notes .

1. Vols. I–IV (Oxford University Press, 1961–62).
2. In the collective article "Man and the notion of history in the East," *Cahiers d'histoire mondiale*, VII, 4 (1963), p. 870.
3. John K. Fairbank, Edwin O. Reischauer, and Albert M. Craig, *East Asia. The Modern Transformation* (Boston, Houghton Mifflin, 1965), p. 9.
4. "Approaches to history in the late nineteenth and early twentieth century Muslim India," *Cahiers d'histoire mondiale*, IX, 4 (1966), p. 987.

ORIENTALISM
&
HISTORY

THE ANCIENT NEAR EAST

WHATEVER geographical meaning may be attached to the "Near East", the "Ancient Near East" is a historical concept. It denotes the extent, in space and time, of the earliest civilised societies. Even before these had arisen momentous advances in man's development had taken place in the same area, among them the change from food-gathering to food-production. The wild forms of emmer wheat and barley are found in Syria and Palestine, and it is probable that in these regions men took the extraordinary step of limiting the satisfaction of immediate needs by saving seeds and storing and protecting them against rodents and insects in order to convey them to the soil at a chosen time; and furthermore, of transforming the wild grasses to the much more nutritious grains by selection and cross-breeding. We know that men living on the slope of Mount Carmel towards the end of the Old Stone Age—perhaps about 8,000–6,000 B.C.—harvested (if they did not cultivate) grain. For they used sickles consisting of short pieces of flint mounted in a bone haft. The same ingenious tools were found with the charred remains of grain in the earliest settlements of Egypt and Mesopotamia, and the flint sickle "teeth" occur in Anatolia and Southern Russia, on the Danube and throughout North Africa, and as far West as Almeria in Spain. In other words the diffusion of agriculture from the Near East did not consist in the spreading of the knowledge of grains alone, but also of a specific technique of harvesting, and presumably of cultivation.

The study of these events concerns the prehistorian rather than the orientalist, and the same is true of several other important inventions which have probably been made within the Near East: the domestication of animals, potting, weaving, and building with sun-dried bricks. The orientalist takes up

1

the story with the great change which set the Ancient Near East apart from the peasant cultures of Eurasia and Africa. It occurred towards 3,000 B.C., in Mesopotamia and in Egypt. New types of polity were created; writing was invented; monumental architecture and sculpture were introduced to express novel conceptions of society's relation to the super-human; social life became civic life.

The changes in Egypt followed those in Mesopotamia but with very little difference in time. And while it is certain that the two countries were in contact, there is no question of slavish imitation. The Mesopotamian example merely stimulated the native inventiveness of the Egyptians. In the course of a few generations the Sumerian and Egyptian civilisations crystallised, each with its own distinctive qualities present *in nuce*. The phenomenon is largely inexplicable, as are most phenomena of individuation. It was an astonishing achievement, this change to a civilised way of life, and for once we are certain that it was a spontaneous change. For the universal level of prehistoric peasant culture had not been passed anywhere else. All the elements of civilisation emerged in two different modes, one Egyptian, the other Mesopotamian; and it remained characteristic for the Ancient Near East that it possessed at all times two distinct and equivalent cultural centres, which were totally different in spirit. They influenced the adjacent regions to such an extent that the civilisations of Syria, Asia Minor and Persia may be considered peripheral to those of the two great river valleys. The peripheral regions took about a thousand years to effect a break with their prehistoric past. The Indus valley, on the other hand, became the seat of a high civilisation by the middle of the third millennium, but its growth and its decay escape us and its inscriptions cannot be read. In the West, Crete became the centre of a remarkably individual civilisation about 2,000 B.C. which, within the next four or five centuries, took root on the Greek mainland.

In area the Ancient Near East stretched, therefore, from Greece to Iran, with an offshoot in the Indus Valley. In time it extended from the second half of the fourth millennium B.C. to the reign of Alexander the Great. One could put the terminal date somewhat earlier, about 500 B.C., when the creative centre of the civilised world had shifted from the Near East to Greece, but it is more logical to include the Achaemenian Empire. In any case the Ancient Near East occupies a distinct position between the universal barbarism of prehistory and classical antiquity.

It is not only this clearly defined position in history which establishes the Ancient Near East as a historical entity. The histories of its peoples show a single rhythm. Connected events caused catastrophes and periods of decline throughout the region. From the middle of the second millennium B.C. onward these histories were actually interlocked. Yet the coherence of the Ancient Near East is one of fortune rather than of origin, imposed by events rather than evolved from within, and in that respect very different from such a historical entity as Europe. There was nothing in the Ancient Near East corresponding with the common heritage of Europe. There was no equivalent of the community of Christendom; of the social order of feudalism; of such basic conceptions as the Holy Roman Empire. There was no universal vehicle of intercourse like Latin, nor any other common classical tradition comparable to that which lives in the art and literature, the learning and superstition of all Europe. In both Egypt and Mesopotamia one recognises something like national classical traditions, but these were not normative for the rest of the Ancient Near East. They affected fitfully and at different times the peripheral regions. Certain features common to the whole of the Ancient Near East are not distinctive since they occur also at other times and places, in fact wherever the achievements of Hellas are unknown. This applies, for instance, to the dominance of mythopoeic and the absence of scientific, critical thought; and to the dominance of ideoplastic and the absence of illusionistic art. A distinctive common culture did not begin to prevail throughout the Near East until Hellenistic times, when it lost its independence and became absorbed in a world centred in the West. This cosmopolitanism was established by the founding of *poleis*, but the ground was already prepared by earlier developments. National particularism had been broken down by the deportation of subject peoples which the Assyrian kings had practised on a large scale. They did not attempt to replace the living cultures they destroyed, but their Persian successors did make such an attempt. The Achaemenian empire resembled that of Charlemagne and Charles V in being a huge political structure, within which cultural assimilation proceeded apace, with the Aramaic language playing to some extent the rôle of Latin. Yet it was only in Hellenistic times that the cosmopolitan began to outstrip the national, local elements in importance.

*   *   *

The cradle of Mesopotamian civilisation was the southern-most part of the Tigris and Euphrates Valley. The earliest settlers of this marshy plain had descended from the highlands of south-west Persia, as we know from their pottery, found beneath the foundations of such cities as Eridu, Ur and Uruk (Erech). At the time of their arrival prehistoric farmers were settled along the middle and upper courses of the two rivers, and the cultural level of the newcomers in the south did not differ from that of their neighbours. But it was in their part of the country that the first cities subsequently arose and this circumstance, together with a certain continuity of culture, makes it probable, as I think, that the earliest villagers from Eridu, Ur and other places in the south, were Sumerians, the creators of Mesopotamian civilisation. In the absence of writing this contention cannot be proved since the hall-mark of the Sumerians is their very remarkable language. It was agglutinative, not flectional, and remains curiously isolated, for it has hitherto proved impossible to bring it into relation with any known tongue. Suggested affinities range from Turkish to Dravidian, from the "Japhetite" languages of the Caucasus to African languages like Bantu and Bornu.

The physical affinities of the Sumerians are less enigmatic. They belonged to the Mediterranean or Brown Race, as is demonstrated by a considerable series of skeletons, dating from the earliest settlements in the south to the latter half of the third millennium B.C. and thus representing the *floruit* of Sumerian culture. It is not to be assumed that this population was "racially pure"—in fact it was similar to that which inhabited Mesopotamia at other times in that it was preponderantly dolichocephalic with a sprinkling of brachycephalics due to perennial infiltration of mountaineers from the North and North-East. But it shows that the physique of the Sumerians did not differ to any measurable extent from that of their neighbours in Syria who spoke a Semitic language.

The high civilisation of the Sumerian South, which came into being before 3,000 B.C., deeply affected the Semitic speaking populations along the middle courses of the Tigris and Euphrates. The objects found in their settlements at Assur and Mari show that they had to a large extent assimilated Sumerian culture. Moreover, the focus of civilisation in the South actually attracted them and by the middle of the 24th century B.C. their immigration had assumed such proportions that one of them, Sargon, became ruler, first of the city of Akkad, then of the whole land. His dynasty ruled for over a century. Semitic Akkadian appeared alongside Sumerian in official and private documents. The Sumerians recovered the hegemony for a few centuries, but they never received reinforcements, while immigration from Syria was continuous and sometimes assumed massive proportions. Soon after 2,000 B.C. the Amorite invasion (which brought the ancestors of Hammurabi to Babylon) finally destroyed the precarious equilibrium. The Sumerians were absorbed by their Semitic speaking countrymen and their speech was only preserved as a sacred language. But the Sumerian epics, liturgies, omens and books of wisdom remained the classical texts of both Babylonians and Assyrians, whether in Akkadian translations or in Sumerian.

It is as yet impossible to decide whether or not the adoption of Sumerian cultural traditions by people of a different origin and speaking a flectional language led to distortions and misinterpretations. This question does not arise in connection with other ethnic groups which immigrated in a continuous trickle or, in times of unrest, in large groups. These mountaineers—Subaraens, Elamites, Hurrians and Kassites—speaking languages which were neither Indo-european nor

Semitic, were thoroughly absorbed by the native culture of the Plain of the two Rivers and do not seem to have affected its character in any way.

In Egypt the cultural continuity was even stronger than in Mesopotamia. There was never any change corresponding with the displacement of Sumerian by Akkadian in Mesopotamia. Egypt seems from the first to have had a homogeneous population of African, notably Hamitic, affinity, and Ancient Egyptian seems to be a basically Hamitic language. It is uncertain whether the many similarities with Semitic usage are due to admixture or to a primordial unity, a common root, of the Hamitic and Semitic languages. Certain peculiarities of Ancient Egyptian culture—for instance a tendency to dualistic thought which comprehends totality as an equilibrium of two opposites; the specifically Egyptian form of divine kingship; and, in early times, the non-utilitarian, emotional significance of cattle—recur among modern East Africans. But the one-sidedness of these modern peoples must not be projected into the past. Neither in Egypt nor in Mesopotamia is there any trace of nomadism as opposed to farming or of a form of agriculture which excludes the keeping of cattle. On the contrary, we find in both countries, even in prehistoric times, evidence of a well-balanced mixed economy in which agriculture and stockbreeding existed side by side and were supplemented by fishing, fowling and hunting.

In both countries the problem of drainage was at first as important as that of irrigation and when, towards 3,000 B.C., political units of an unprecedented scope came into being, the reclamation of marsh land and the regulation and distribution of water likewise assumed entirely new proportions.

*   *   *

The earliest indications of the momentous changes to which I have alluded, are archaeological. Mesopotamian ruins of the end of the 4th millennium B.C. derive from settlements large enough to be called cities and containing public buildings on a scale not met before. These early cities centred round one or more shrines and records of a somewhat later period throw light on the relationship between temple and city; it was one of manor and estate. A god in whom the community projected its sovereignty as well as its hopes, owned the land and its produce. The temple was not merely a place of worship but the centre of a large administration, with its own offices, storehouses and workshops. The functioning of this apparatus was made possible by the invention of writing, an invention which—whatever its vast consequences—served at first merely the practical requirements of the temple organisation. The tablets with the earliest writing in existence are wage lists, inventories, receipts and similar documents. The signs are either pictograms or abstract symbols, like the circle with a cross which stands for "sheep", one of the commonest entries. But before long the ideogrammatic notation was supplemented by phonetic signs. And once the principle of representing sounds was recognised, writing as a rendering of language had become possible. The principle was not applied consistently (ideograms remained in use) and the script was cumbersome in the extreme, even after the original signs had been transformed into groups of wedges impressed by a stylus in the clay of the tablets (hence the name cuneiform script). Yet this awkward and often ambiguous device was the fountainhead of all subsequent development, from Egyptian hieroglyphs to the Greek alphabet. It is, at present, uncertain whether Chinese writing and the Indus script are also in some way connected with early Sumerian writing.

The form of the new society which built the earliest cities has been described as "theocratic socialism." Its basis was "mixed farming", or rather the many-sided balanced economy to which I have referred when describing prehistoric conditions. But the founding of cities brought an intensification of communal life in all its manifestations. There was a differentiation of professions (although almost all citizens remained practical farmers) and an extension of external contacts. Copper had been used in prehistoric times but it was now required for a large variety of tools, vessels and weapons. Silver, lead and gold were also needed, as well as various stones, from the coarse ones used for handmills to the semi-precious stones embellishing ritual objects and personal ornaments. But all these materials had to be imported; the plain produced only food and wool. The merchants who travelled abroad to barter metals and other minerals remained members of the temple community and traded on its behalf, although here, as in the case of craftsmen, shepherds, and most other classes of people, the "planned economy" was surrounded by a fringe of legitimate private enterprise which remained free. Yet the merchant, like every other citizen, received an allotment of the god's land to cultivate for his sustenance.

These traders brought lapis lazuli from Afghanistan, copper and silver from Armenia and Anatolia, stud-animals from Elam. The technical skills developed in the new cities and organised on a larger scale than ever before, made it possible to use manufactured goods, less bulky and more highly prized than food-stuffs, for barter. Through the export of rugs and textiles, weapons, jewelry and the like, the influence of Sumerian civilisation permeated the whole of the Ancient Near East. Engraved gold vases of Sumerian design have been found at Astrabad near the Caspian Sea; early inscribed tablets at Sialk near Kashan; seals of cylindrical shape of Mesopotamian design have turned up at Troy, on the Cyclades, in Syria and in Egypt; Sumerian types of weapons and ornaments in Persia, North Syria and the Caucasus.

In its homeland Mesopotamian civilisation suffered from the limitations of its political conceptions. Originally the autonomy of the city under its divine owner was absolute, and no larger unit ever acquired a comparable sanction. At first the city-state seemed to have known an assembly of citizens but already in early times power was concentrated in a monarch elected by the god. The office fell either to the High Priest of the city god, or to a *lugal*, literally a Great Man, designated to wield absolute power during an emergency; but conflicts between the expanding city-states tended to become chronic and the office of *lugal* became often permanent. The dynastic principle was prevalent in practice but not in theory since the assembly of the gods, acting through the city god, predestined or elected an individual for rulership. They granted him occasionally supremacy over the whole land, and the Akkadians attempted to supersede local patriotism by the acknowledgement of a national unity which was essential if the rich cities of the plain, exposed to the depredations of mountaineers and desert dwellers, should safeguard their existence. Yet the national state disintegrated time and again through the defection of the cities; even in the first millennium when the Assyrians held the country in an iron grip, the king had annually to interrupt his campaigns in Armenia or Syria to go to Babylon, the spiritual centre of Western Asia, "to take the hands of the god Bel" at the New Year's Festival, a ceremony which had sanctioned the authority of the ruler of that city since time immemorial.

Yet society had become increasingly secular. There is documentary evidence, dated soon after 2,000 B.C., for private ownership of land. The merchants became independent and organised trade on remarkably efficient lines. They founded companies for trading abroad and developed banking; they were backed by courts under the king's authority which required properly witnessed evidence of loans, sales and contracts. Thousands of clay tablets referring to legal and business matters have been preserved. Several law codes, of which one promulgated by Hammurabi of Babylon is the most famous, have likewise been recovered.

*　　*　　*

In Egypt a totally different society came into being. At the time when the earliest cities were founded in Sumer, a large part of Upper Egypt was united under a house of divine kings, in each of whom the sky-god Horus—also manifest as a falcon—was believed to be incarnate. The Wady Hammamat which leads from the Red Sea to the Nile Valley ended in their domain, and it was probably along this route that the expanding Sumerians made contact with the Egyptians. Mesopotamian cylinder-seals have been found in Upper Egypt and monuments of the early Horus kings were decorated with designs of Mesopotamian origin. The earliest monumental architecture of Egypt consists of royal tombs of mud brick which follow, in design and technical details, Sumerian usage. Hieroglyphic writing shows a combination of ideograms and phonetic signs which is characteristic for Sumerian writing at the time of contact, and it is possible that this contact suggested

the possibility of writing to the Egyptians. But the two
scripts have nothing in common. Those great innovations were not, however, confined to
Upper Egypt. For at this time—perhaps about 3,100 B.C.
—the Horus kings united the country from the first cataract
up to the mouths of the Nile, and the Egyptians clearly
recognised this event—which may have actually been the work
of two or three generations—as the beginning of their history
by attributing it to a first king of a first dynasty. The contrast
with Mesopotamia is complete; there the country was strewn
with a number of autonomous cities whose separate histories
were only later, and rather imperfectly, joined. Egypt comes
into being as a united royal domain, rural in character, with
cities which were important merely as religious centres. The
country even lacked, until the second millennium B.C., a
permanent capital. In Mesopotamia the earliest texts were
economic and administrative documents, in Egypt they were
records or memorials of the kings' achievements. Not that
economic matters were neglected : for one of the earliest
reliefs shows Pharaoh opening a canal, and annual records of
the height of the Nile were kept even during the first dynasty,
no doubt for the purpose of estimating revenue.

The administration was centralised to an extreme degree,
and the highest officials were relatives of the king. Travelling
agents of the court—called "The eyes and the ears of Pharaoh"
—continually visted local officials to gather their reports or to
transmit orders to them. Egypt, like Mesopotamia, required
minerals and other raw materials from abroad, but these
were obtained through royal expeditions, not through private
trade. The treasury equipped and staffed armies of labourers
and soldiers to mine copper, malachite and turquoise in Sinai,
or stone in the Eastern desert; or to bring gold, ivory, ebony,
precious skins and ostrich feathers from the Sudan. Royal
fleets went to Byblos at the foot of the Lebanon to fetch the
large quantities of good timber which the acacias, sycamores
and palm trees of Egypt could not supply. Wine and olive
oil were fetched from Libya and Palestine, and later imported
from Crete. The distribution of these materials started at
the top of the social pyramid, in the form of rations and

rewards to the court officials, hence to their suites, and so on to the village headman and the craftsmen of the country estates.

The paradox that in the person of Pharaoh, the living king, a god had taken charge of the nation retained its validity until the end of the second millennium B.C. It was very rarely challenged, partly because the surrounding deserts could not support powerful neighbours. Twice the established order was temporarily destroyed. In the 22nd century B.C. the Old Kingdom, after some centuries of extraordinary achievements, collapsed in disorder. And in the 18th century B.C. a mixed horde of Asiatics, the Hyksos or "Shepherd Kings", overran lower Egypt. This episode burnt itself in the memory of the Egyptians, and when the barbarians were driven out, they were pursued with such vehemence that Palestine and Syria were occupied. The occupation was not permanent, but was made so in subsequent reigns, and a more intimate contact with the Levant than the trade of earlier times had brought about, was thereby established. At times Egyptian influence reached as far East as the Upper Euphrates, although normally the Syrian hinterland was a Mesopotamian sphere of influence. Throughout Palestine and Syria there were small kingdoms and principalities, sometimes extensive, sometimes hardly more than fortified towns with their surrounding fields; the rulers were vassals of whichever great power happened to be predominant in the region. The local courts often aped Egyptian usages (as engraved ivories show) exactly as in the 8th and 7th centuries B.C. the North Syrian princelings conformed to Assyrian court usage.

By about 1,900 B.C. the situation had become more complex than it had been before. The invasion of the Egyptian delta by the Hyksos had been part of a widespread movement of peoples which had carried the Hurrians into North Syria and North-Eastern Iraq, the Hittites into Asia Minor and the Mitanni into Syria. The Hurrians gained neither political nor cultural importance. The Mitanni were true Aryans, speaking a Satem language and worshipping such Indian gods as Indra, Mitra and Varuna. They were great trainers of horses, and their cavalry (consisting of light war chariots with a span of horses, not mounted soldiers) made them a power in Syria and as far East as Kirkuk beyond the Tigris. The Hittites had settled at the same time in Asia Minor; this people contained also elements speaking Indo-European languages, but they used either a peculiar hieroglyphic or the Mesopotamian cuneiform script. In the archives found at their capital eight languages are represented, including Sumerian and Akkadian. The Hittites overpowered the Mitanni and were strong enough to enforce the loyalty of Levantine princes who had previously been vassals of Egypt or Babylonia.

In Crete a brilliant civilisation had come into flower by the 18th century B.C. By 1,600 B.C. it had penetrated into the Peloponnese and the Argolid, where it was adopted by local princelings—at Mycenae, Argos and Pylos—who themselves had arrived with their followers in the course of earlier popular movements. By 1,400 these mainlanders occupied part of Crete, and the recent decipherment of Cretan linear B script has proved that these people were Greeks. A little later, probably in the 13th century B.C., the Hebrews who had for some time moved through Transjordan and the Southern desert, occupied Palestine.

During the first half of the second millennium a larger area and more peoples than ever before reached a high level of culture. Up to about 1,200 B.C. the history of the Ancient Near East can be summarised in two phases; the emergence of the first great civilisations in Mesopotamia and Egypt; thereafter, the gradual but increasing involvement of the peripheral in the civilising process which derived its force from the two great river valleys.

But about 1,200 B.C. new waves of peoples swept through Asia Minor and the Levant, destroying the Hittite empire and nearly wrecking Egypt. After this ordeal the creative power of the Ancient Near East appears diminished. In some fields—for instance in Assyrian astronomy—important advances were still made. But in the main we observe a codification and consolidation of acquired knowledge.

*   *   *

Without returning to an outmoded point of view which perversely considered the Ancient Near Eastern achievement as a prelude to that of Hellas, one must admit that the final stage of the history of the Ancient Near East acquires a special significance from the fact that the Greeks found in it a source of knowledge and inspiration. The transmission of Ancient Near Eastern knowledge and usage to the West is, in fact, an aspect of our subject which is of particular interest to the general historian. But it is unexpectedly difficult to assess the indebtedness of the Greeks to their neighbours in the East and South, partly because of the high originality of their spirit which transformed whatever it borrowed, and partly because of the complexity of the factors involved. There is, on the one hand, the multiplicity of the Ancient Near Eastern elements which has, I hope, become clear in these pages; and, on the other hand, it is often difficult to decide whether signs of Near Eastern influence in classical sources represent early or late, notably Hellenistic, derivations. The process of transmission is therefore more obscure than the many known facts would lead one to suspect. It is simple enough to state that the division of the day into 24 hours, or of the circle into 360°, derives from Babylonia, or that the Egyptians knew a convenient year of 12 months of 30 days each, with 5 epagomenal days. The dependence of early Greek sculpture on Egypt is as obvious as the dependence of Hellenistic astrology on Mesopotamia. The centaur and the faun, and Herakles' destruction of the Hydra with the help of Iolaus, have prototypes in Sumerian art. The theogony of Hesiod reflects Ancient Near Eastern beliefs as clearly as do the cults of Demeter or Adonis. There is a Hittite prototype for the maiming of Uranos by Kronos. This list could easily be extended, but there remains to be found a point of view which imparts coherence to these multifarious facts.

The general historian who would contribute to a solution of this problem can now rely on an invaluable collection of up-to-date translations.[1] There are, likewise, critical and

---

[1] *Ancient Near Eastern Texts relating to the Old Testament*, edited by James B. Pritchard, Princeton, 1950.

up-to-date histories of Egypt[2] and of the Hittites.[3] Oddly enough no similar history of Mesopotamia is available, probably because of the chronological controversies which are still raging. It is, however, well to remember that the divergencies of view are insignificant compared with those existing but a short time ago. It is impossible to discuss here the material upon which the discussions are based.[4] It consists of lists of kings and reigns, and of a few astronomical points of reference. The lists are apt to become less trustworthy the further the facts recorded are removed from the lifetime of the compiler. But of recent years a vast body of complementary evidence has become available. Peaceful or war-like contact between the various countries has left its traces either in written documents, often dated in definite reigns, or in importations recovered in stratified deposits which can be more or less precisely dated. No chronological system based on evidence from one country alone can henceforth claim to be valid, since the cross-datings supplied by foreign contacts provide a correction to the faultiness or incompleteness of the lists. Thanks to the recent discoveries at Mari (Tell Hariri), Alalakh (Tell Atshana) and Ugarit (Ras Shamra), a particularly dense network of inter-relations throughout the Near East has been established between the 19th and the 14th centuries B.C. It is obvious that a decision taking such material into account can no longer be based on mere computations but includes an evaluation of facts and therefore a margin of personal judgment. But that margin has now become relatively small. The reign of Hammurabi of Babylon is placed by Sidney Smith from 1792–1750 B.C. and by Albrecht Goetze from 1848–1806 B.C. There are two "short chronologies", proposed by W. F. Albright (1728–1686 B.C.) and E. Weidner (1704–1662 B.C.). In my opinion these are unlikely to be correct. Any decision entails a corresponding arrangement of the dates for the third millennium B.C.

---

[2] *L'Egypte*, par Étienne Drioton et Jacques Vandier ("Clio," Introduction aux études historiques), Paris, 1938.

[3] *The Hittites*, by O. R. Gurney (Pelican Books A 259), Harmondsworth, Middlesex, 1952.

[4] But see *Archéologie Mésopotamienne*, II, *Technique et Problèmes* by André Parrot, Paris, 1953.

which are established by dead reckoning. Beyond the middle of that millennium they are mere approximations. But it appears then that the present disagreement concerns a period of no more than 50 years, or, as some would say, a century. Much more serious are the uncertainties with which the general historian must reckon, as a result of the incomplete understanding of both grammar and vocabulary of most of the Ancient Near Eastern languages. Ancient Egyptian and Akkadian are relatively well known. The other languages are in varying degrees in process of recovery. Sumerian texts of the greatest importance lie untranslated in museums.

It is impossible for the general historian to ignore the birth of civilisation in the Ancient Near East. But he must know that in approaching this subject he embarks on the crossing of treacherous waters.

✠ H. FRANKFORT.

ISLAM

It has been remarked that the history of the Arabs has been written in Europe chiefly by historians who knew no Arabic, or by Arabists who knew no history. The gibe is sharp, but not wholly unjustified. In most Western universities history and oriental studies are separate disciplines, cultivated by different teachers and students, often with different objectives and methods of study. It would no doubt be an exaggeration to say that the twain never meet—but it would not be unfair to say that they pass each other on the same road with cold and perfunctory greetings, sometimes even with averted eyes.

On the one hand the Orientalist, relying on his philological sword and buckler to strike true and to safeguard him from error, has tackled history and philosophy, art and sociology, literature and economics, with equal readiness and often, alas, with equal competence. On the other hand the historian, trusting in the insight vouchsafed to him by his professional discipline and experience, has not hesitated to deal with mediaeval Spain without Arabic, the Eastern question without Turkish, and the expansion of Europe without any reference to the languages and literatures of the peoples among whom Europe expanded.

For a long time these activities could to some extent be justified, if only by the argument that no other kind was possible in the circumstances of the time. There was not much that the historian could do with Islamic sources, even if he took the trouble to learn some Arabic, Persian, or Turkish, for very many of these sources, including some of the most important, were unexplained, unpublished, even unidentified. A great deal of preliminary work was still needed—to find, describe, and edit texts, to discover, read, and interpret inscriptions, to disinter, publish, and evaluate documents—all in the absence of any but the most general dictionaries and of almost all the basic works of reference such as are at the hand of, for example, the classical or mediaeval historian.

There are still no historical grammars or dictionaries of the languages of Islam, and even the general dictionaries are few and inadequate. There are few works worthy of the name on palaeography, epigraphy, sigillography, diplomatic, and other ancillary sciences. There are few general works of reference even on such matters as biography, topography, and terminology.

In the absence of all these aids to scholarship, work on the Islamic historical sources demanded of the researcher an arduous philological discipline, so arduous that it left little time for the further disciplinary training of the historian. Likewise the Western historian was unlikely to get very far even if he were daring enough to take up an oriental language. There is no such thing as a "working knowledge" of an oriental language. To learn one means serious and protracted study, and often, when the historian attempted to use oriental sources in the original, the danger of misunderstanding and misinterpretation probably remained greater than if he had been content to use translations made by Orientalists—though, it may be said in passing, these translations were themselves by no means immune from error.

Here and there isolated figures of genius combined the competence of the oriental philologist with the insight of the historian. But even the others, though lacking this rare combination of skills, nevertheless did necessary and even indispensable work, and if they were sometimes infelicitous in their historical efforts, they still helped to achieve a deeper and more accurate knowledge of Islamic languages, Islamic civilisation, and so ultimately also of Islamic history.

This preliminary work is still far from completed. The published sources are still only the visible tenth of the iceberg protruding above the surface of the waters, while the mass remains below, a danger to the unwary. Many texts, inscriptions, and, above all, documents still await edition or re-edition. Lexicography and the historical auxiliary sciences are still at a very immature stage of development. But even so, sufficient progress has been made to allow, even to require, the emergence of oriental history as a separate discipline within oriental studies, and furthermore to give to the non-Orientalist

historian the possibility of securing a very much better knowledge of Islamic history than has hitherto been possible.

Such knowledge is a necessity for the historian, not only
because of the intrinsic value and interest of Islamic history
in itself as an important and significant part of the history of
the human race, but also because of the many points of contact
and overlap between the history of Islam and the history of
other civilisations, which cannot be fully studied and understood without reference to Islamic history and even to Islamic
sources.

*   *   *

Before we discuss this point further, it may be useful to
attempt some definition of the extent of the subject in space
and time and also of its content.

The scope of our enquiry is the history of Islam; that is to
say, of the peoples, societies and states that accepted the faith
and law of Islam and professed to live by them. The story
begins with the career of the Prophet Muhammad in Arabia
in the early 7th century. Its first chapters deal with his
preaching in Mecca, his migration from Mecca to Medina
that forms the starting point of the Muslim era, and the creation
of the first Muslim state in Medina. It continues with the
religious and political unification of the Arabs of the peninsula
and with the great movement of Arab Islamic expansion. In
successive waves of conquest, Islam spread over Arabia, spilt
beyond the desert borders into the Fertile Crescent, then eastward across Persia to Central Asia, westward across North
Africa to the Atlantic. From this vast extent of territory,
embracing many ancient centres of civilisation, new impulses
of conquest again carried Islam into Europe at many points :
from the far west, through Spain over the Pyrenees and half-
way across France; in the centre, from Tunis to Sicily and from
Sicily to southern Italy, groping northwards into the Alpine
passes; in the east, into Asia Minor and thence branching both
into the Balkans and into the Caucasus and further still into
Central Europe and the broad steppes of what is now southern
Russia. And along the whole line, too, there was an expansion
southwards :—beyond the Sahara, ever deeper into tropical
Africa; across the mountain passes and the eastern seas to India,

to Malaya, and to the East Indies, while at the same time
other incursions carried the creed of Islam into China and the
northern reaches of Asia.

This vast zone contains a great diversity of peoples. Some
of them, as in Africa, were barbarians who found in Islam
their first taste of civilisation; others were peoples of ancient
civilisation, with deep-rooted traditions of religion, politics, and
culture; but all of them were moulded into the common
civilisation of Islam. For despite its important local diversities,
Islam succeeded in imposing on all the peoples who accepted
it the basic stamp of unity.

This unity rests, in the first instance, on the Islamic faith,
the common creed of all Muslims, then on the law, the holy
law of Islam which, despite much local variation of custom,
remains the common ideal pattern of belief and conduct for
the whole Muslim world. The political traditions of Muslims
everywhere were shaped by memories of the Caliphate and
of the Sultanate of old Islam and by the formulations of the
Muslim jurists, while even political practice was much
influenced by the common experience of the great Muslim
Empires. The literary culture of all these countries was
profoundly influenced by the Arabic language, the holy tongue
of Islam, the language of the Qur'ān and of the traditions of
the Prophet. Almost all Muslim languages are, or were
formerly, written in the Arabic script, and most of them have
borrowed great numbers of Arabic words, especially in two
fields which, for the Muslim, are closely connected : the one
of matters relating to religion and philosophy and to spiritual
and intellectual life generally, the other of matters relating to
law and government, and to social and political life.

The originality and authenticity of Islamic civilisation can
nowhere be seen more clearly than in its arts and architecture—
in the unmistakable Islamic stamp on buildings and artifacts
from Morocco to the Java seas which, despite so many persistent
and divergent local traditions, proclaims the unity and identity
of the Islamic cultural pattern. Even in those countries like
Spain and Sicily, where the Muslim faith has been uprooted
and ejected, and with it most of the intellectual and spiritual
heritage of Islam, something remains of the arts of Islam—in

the graceful lines of Saracenic architecture, the formalised fantasies of the arabesque, the decorative use of calligraphy and geometrical design on friezes and textiles. The debt of South European agriculture and irrigation to the Moors is attested by their vocabulary and nomenclature. Even in the song and dance of southern Spain some echoes and traces may be discerned of oriental rhythms.

Inside the Islamic world, the unity of faith, law, script, and tradition was maintained and reinforced by extensive circulation between the various different countries and especially by the annual pilgrimage, which brought Muslims from the whole vast territory of Islam to the common goal in Mecca.

The heart of the Islamic world is the Near and Middle East, comprising, in order of Islamisation, Arabia, the Fertile Crescent and Egypt, Persia and Turkey. This region shows certain geographical features which have important social and cultural consequences. The most striking geographical characteristic of the whole area is the presence of great deserts in all the lands of Arabic speech and most of the lands of Turkish and Persian speech. The contrast in the Middle East between the desert and the sown has led to a division between nomads and cultivators, between stock-raisers and peasants, that finds its earliest expression in the story of Cain and Abel and may be still seen in the present discord between bedouin and fellah.

The great river valleys are another striking characteristic. The two main centres of civilisation in the region, Egypt and Iraq, are essentially river valleys. Both have societies of great antiquity based on artificial irrigation, requiring large numbers of skilled workmen controlled by a strong central authority. This need led to the growth of a centralised, authoritarian and bureaucratic form of government and to a system of political thought and practice based upon it.

A third factor that has had a determining effect in Middle Eastern history is the trade routes. During long periods the Middle East has carried the trade routes between the Mediterranean and the Western world on the one hand, and India, China, and South East Asia on the other. The main routes have run through Egypt to the Red Sea, through the valleys of the Tigris and Euphrates to the Persian Gulf, and across Persia to the overland routes to China and India.

The general economic structure of the region has been based on a peasant agriculture depending in most areas on artificial irrigation. The raising of animals for food and transport was left to the nomads of the desert, who, in certain periods of political weakness, played a vital role. But, for all that, Islam is not a desert religion as has sometimes been asserted, nor is it a fellah religion as Spengler would have it. It is essentially a culture of cities. It was born in the trading town of Mecca, grew to adolescence in the town of Medina and reached maturity in the great urban centres of the Middle East—Damascus, Bagdad, and Cairo, then Isfahan, Constantinople, Bukhara and Qairawan, Samarkand and Cordoba. The Islamic town began as a military cantonment, became a market and finally evolved into a centre of diversified urban civilisation.

Islam is one of the great religions of mankind and has in the past attracted to itself hundreds of millions of men in the central bloc of the Eastern Hemisphere, most of whose descendants still live by Islamic faith and tradition. Within this faith and tradition a rich literature grew up, in many forms and in many languages. The Persian poets are probably the best known Islamic writers outside the Islamic world. But other writers of prose and poetry arose in Arabic, Turkish, and other languages, whose works are not unworthy of attention. In this Islamic civilisation were united, for the first time in history, the vast territories stretching from the borders of India and China to the approaches of Greece, Italy and France. For a while by their military and political power, for much longer by their faith, law, and culture, the Muslims brought and kept together in a single society two formerly conflicting worlds—the millenial and diversified Mediterranean tradition of Rome, Greece, Israel, and the ancient Near East, and the rich and original civilisation of Persia, with its own different pattern of life, thought, and sentiment, and its fruitful contacts with the great civilisations of the remoter East. For a brief but splendid period the

Islamic world was the centre of scientific and philosophic progress, and its scholars—men of many races and religions— played a vital role as intermediaries, preserving and transmitting to Christian Europe something of the heritage of Greek antiquity, enriched and augmented by their own efforts and also by their borrowings and adaptations from further East. Chinese paper and Indian numerals both reached Europe via the Arabs, by whose name the latter are still erroneously called. They were a gift not unworthy of comparison with the philosophy of Aristotle and the medicine of Galen, in their effect on the rise of European science and scholarship.

Perhaps the greatest, or at least the most characteristic, creation of Islamic civilisation is in the visual arts, more especially in the decorative and industrial arts and in architecture. These reflect in their different facets both the eclecticism and the originality of Islamic civilisation, the continuity and unity of its tradition, the extent of its influence. In the paintings that adorn the walls of the Arab castles of Syria, in the artifacts excavated in the Arab garrision cities and capitals in Iraq and Egypt, we can see how the conquerors first acquired the works of art—and even the artists—of other civilisations, then imitated them separately, and finally fused them into something new, authentic, and original. From the 9th century onwards, the rise of new ruling classes of Persian and Turkish origin brought new tastes and new skills. In the pottery of Iraq, for example, we find, together with objects in Byzantine and Sasanid style, imported articles from China, local imitations of them, and new creations evolved by experiment with old and new, native and foreign models. Lustred pottery and calligraphic decoration, the Persian arch and the stalactite pendentive spread westwards to Spain and eastwards to India as typical and universal expressions of Islamic aesthetic sensibility.

*   *   *

Islamic civilisation thus forms an interesting and significant subject of study for itself—but not only for itself. Its wide extent, its many contacts, its civilising rôle and its rich documentation make it important for many other fields.

Let us first consider European history. The great clash between Christendom and Islam in the Crusades has for long been one of the major concerns of the mediaeval historian. Yet to this day Western scholars have studied it almost entirely on the basis of western sources, supplemented by such few oriental works—most of them late and secondary—as are available in translations—most of them incomplete and inaccurate. Even such outstanding figures as Saladin still await serious monographs—still more so the numerous other Muslim protagonists of the drama. In Western Europe itself, important areas were for centuries under Muslim rule and formed centres of Muslim culture. The Caliphate of Cordoba and the Amirate of Palermo are parts of European history, which cannot be fully understood without them. The Muslim regimes of Spain and Sicily are important not only because of the European territories over which they ruled, but also because of the influence which they exerted on the rest of Europe, on the many English, French, Italian, German, and other Europeans who went to Moorish Spain and Sicily to study and to translate, and who, by bringing ancient and eastern scientific and philosophical works into the sphere of knowledge of the Western world, started a kind of renaissance in the 12th century. All this is usually studied only from Western sources. But Arabic literature can still add much to our knowledge of European history in this respect.

Muslim rule in Europe is not by any means limited to the West. In Eastern Europe too there were areas of Muslim rule and influence. The Mongol conquerors were not Muslims, but they were soon Islamised and moreover had under them great numbers of Muslim Turks, especially from the Turkish peoples variously known as Kipchaks or Polovtzi. The Khanate of the Golden Horde which ruled for centuries over much of Russia was a Muslim state of a sort, and after its collapse it left lesser Muslim states and principalities for a very much longer period in the Crimea, north of the Caucasus and along the Volga.

Most important of all the Muslim incursions into Europe in view of their duration and long-term effects were those of the Ottoman Turks in the South-East from the 14th century onwards. The Ottoman conquests brought great areas of Europe under Muslim rule, in Greece, the Balkans, and as far as Hungary and Poland. Most European history books give a grossly distorted picture of Ottoman rule in these countries and of its effects, which is based on exclusively western and often rather flimsy evidence, and they in general sadly misrepresent the rôle of the Turks in European history.

Europe is the area of Islamic expansion with which we, as Europeans, are most directly concerned. But European history is by no means the only field of study that marches with that of Islam. India and Indonesia were both important areas of Islamic expansion and the seats of great Islamic civilisations. New Islamic languages and literatures, kingdoms and empires arose there, all of which for their full understanding require some knowledge of the Middle Eastern Islamic background from which the conquering faith came. Middle Eastern Islam not only provided the initial impulse but also continued to maintain contacts with many of these remoter civilisations—contacts which have often left important documentation. Arab travellers and geographers have much to tell us of India and South-East Asia. Ottoman sources, both chronicles and documents, contain useful information on the great struggle of the Europeans, chiefly the Portuguese and Dutch, against Islamic powers in Asia from the Red Sea coast of Africa to Sumatra. The Ottomans also maintained intermittent diplomatic relations with a number of Muslim states in India. These can be followed in the chronicles and more especially in the Ottoman archives. Published documents from Turkish records include correspondence between the Ottomans and various Moghul emperors of India as well as later rulers like Tipu Sahib. Even in China, the historian may still need to refer to Islamic sources. There was an extensive Muslim trade with the Far East going both overland via Central Asia and by sea to the China coast, and dating back to the 8th century. It has left many traces in Arabic and Persian literature.

A new field of historical studies to which more and more attention is being given nowadays is the history of tropical

Africa before the colonial era. To a large extent this depends on archaeological evidence and oral tradition. The deficiencies of this kind of material, in particular the difficulty of fitting it into a chronological framework, give special value to such odd scraps of dated information as can be found in external sources. For the period before the coming of the white man to tropical Africa these are almost exclusively Muslim. From early Islamic times, Arab traders in search of slaves and gold penetrated deep into tropical Africa :—from Egypt to the Sudan, Abyssinia, and beyond; from Arabia and Persia by sea to the East coast; from the Barbary States across the Sahara to Central Africa, the Guinea Coast, and the West. Much valuable information concerning tropical Africa and its peoples is scattered through Arabic works on geography and travel, in the many writings concerning slaves and the slave trade, and in the still largely unpublished literature of the Sultanate of Morocco with its many references to Moorish expeditions to the South and dealings with Negro chiefs and princes.

*   *   *

The scope of Islamic history is, then, vast and offers a boundless range of possible interest and information to specialists in other fields. But how far is this information accessible; to what extent are the sources available and intelligible ?

We may divide the internal sources for Islamic history into two main groups—the literary and the documentary.

I. Literary

The Islamic peoples produced a immense number of literary works of all kinds, almost all of them of some potential value to the historian. The most important are of course the chronicles. These are present in great quantity for almost every place and period. Islamic societies, from the first, have always been conscious of their place in history—Islamic rulers have been interested in the deeds of their predecessors, and have desired to record their own for the sake of their successors. Islamic historiography began with the careful recording by pious men of the acts and sayings of the Prophet, of his companions, and of his immediate successors. Thereafter almost every dynasty in Islam had annals of some kind. In some countries—as in India—reliable historiography begins with the Islamic invasion. These chronicles are very limited in many respects, but taken as a whole they constitute an enormously valuable source of knowledge. The earliest chronicles are not continuous records but collections of eye-witness accounts each introduced by a chain of authorities. Then come the annals of the Empire, universal histories, and a wide range of histories with a more restricted topic as, for example, local histories of towns, provinces, or dynasties, and personal histories such as individual biographies and, more frequently, biographical dictionaries of various classes of individuals. These include companions of the prophet, Qur'ān reciters, poets, literati, physicians, governors, officials, judges and mystics—or simply inhabitants of a certain city. There are even subject histories dealing with such topics as floods, famines, plagues, and wars, or with particular places and events.

At first all these historical works were in Arabic, which was for long the sole language of government and culture of the Muslim state. From the 11th century onwards the use of Arabic for historical works was gradually restricted to the Arabic-speaking countries from Iraq to Spain. A new historical literature appeared in Persian, which became the dominant literary language not only in Persia but also in Turkey, Central Asia, and Muslim India. The third of the three major languages of Islam was Turkish, of which there are several varieties. From the 14th and 15th centuries the Ottoman Turks began what 'developed into a rich Turkish historical literature, while another literature on parallel lines, though on a smaller scale, arose among the Eastern Turks in Central Asia and Afghanistan in the Eastern Turkish or Chaghatay language. It is in this little-known language that one of the greatest masterpieces of Islamic literature, the autobiography of Babur, founder of the Moghul Empire, was written. Then, later, chronicles were written in almost all the other languages of Islam, including such languages as Malay and Javanese at one extremity of the Muslim world, and Swahili and Hausa at the other.

As regards the accessibility of the sources, the situation varies greatly. For the early period, up to about the 10th and 11th centuries A.D., the position is excellent and most of the sources are available, but thereafter there are still appalling gaps. Many of the most important chronicles are still in manuscript, others are available only in defective and inaccurate editions. Of late, the efforts of Middle Eastern and especially of Egyptian scholars have made available in print many chronicles of the Crusades and Mamluk periods. This greatly improves the prospects of study, but much more still remains to be done.

Most of the official Ottoman histories, that is, the writings of the Imperial historiographers, are available in old printed editions produced in Constantinople—some of them dating back to the early 18th century; many other Turkish chronicles are also in print, and a fair number of Persian chronicles have been printed in Persia and the West. But there are still a good many Persian and Turkish chronicles that await their editors. Even one of the greatest of Persian historians, Rashid-ad-Din, the first Muslim historian to write a universal history going beyond the Islamic oecumene, still awaits a complete edition. Generally speaking, while the numbers of texts still awaiting edition are large, many are becoming available since the task of editing them is no longer discharged exclusively by European Orientalists but also—and at the present time far more extensively—by scholars in Islamic countries.

The textual and historical criticism of the chronicles has also made some progress, especially for the early Caliphate, for the Crusades period, and the early Ottoman period; but in this respect the general situation is less satisfactory and far more remains to be done. Translations are very few : adequate ones still fewer. During the 16th and 17th centuries such pioneer translators as Löwenklau and Pococke did work of enormous importance in making some of the sources, and through them some of the facts of Islamic and Ottoman history, available to the European reader. The old translations from the 16th to the 19th centuries are, however, for the most part unreliable; most of them are translated from late and secondary sources which were the first to become known in Europe. Moreover the translations themselves were full of philological and historical errors, most of which were probably inevitable in the state of knowledge of the time. There are some recent translations of Arabic and Persian chronicles, but far from enough. From Turkish there are even fewer. The task of translating such a work is no easy one, requiring far more than a knowledge of the language— and that is rare enough.

II. Documentary Sources

From the period before the 15th century there are very few documentary sources. There are only three groups of any importance. The first consists of the inscriptions, of which there are considerable numbers from all over the Islamic world. Arabic inscriptions of the first few centuries of Islam have been well covered. They have been published in a corpus and in a repertoire, and have been fairly thoroughly studied. Inscriptions in other Muslim languages are comparatively few, since the purpose of most inscriptions was pious, and the language of piety was usually Arabic. The second group consists of the papyri coming from Egypt, together with a very small number from other places. These, too, have been published in great numbers and studied, and have proved a very valuable source of information on early Islamic history in Egypt, particularly in matters of administration and finance. A third group consists of the *Geniza*—a collection of miscellaneous papers and documents, chiefly of the Fatimid period, preserved by the Jews in Cairo and now scattered among different Western libraries.

From the 15th and more especially from the 16th century the Ottoman achives at Istanbul offer a vast mass of source material. Though the great collections preserved in the former Turkish capital are still imperfectly explored, a good start has already been made in rehousing and in cataloguing them, and important groups and classes of documents are now accessible.

In these collections Turkish source materials are available which can illuminate the history of South and South-East

Europe and often of the rest of Europe. The Ottoman Empire was after all for a long time a European Great Power, and its records no less than those of the other European Great Powers are of value for the history of Europe generally. A great mass of records is preserved in the Istanbul Archives and is still untouched. But even such documents as have been published in Turkey by Turkish scholars are not yet known or used in the West. How many Western historians are aware that published Turkish documents include the letters and reports of the Turkish Ambassadors in Paris from 1796–1806, records of the mission of Namik Pasha to London in 1832, the political despatches of Rashid Pasha to his Government during his stay in Paris in 1834–36, countless documents relating to the Turkish attitude to Muhammad 'Ali's regime in Egypt, and the Turkish diplomatic documents of the year 1877 dealing with the Russo-Turkish war and the Treaty of San Stefano? The introduction of Ottoman documents to the common pool of European historical sources is a matter of urgency, for with them much can be illuminated that now remains hidden in darkness, or else is seen in a false or half-light.

I have already referred to some other documents which, with these, may serve as examples of the very much greater quantities that remain. Access to these documents is difficult. They are composed in a highly technical chancery language, written in a series of special scripts presenting unusual problems of decipherment and interpretation; but already important progress has been made. A number of detailed studies of individual documents have been published in Europe, many documents have been published or described in recent years by Turkish scholars. Results cannot yet be said to be available to any serious extent to the non-Orientalist, but these documents must probably be regarded as the greatest single source of historical knowledge of the Islamic world that remains to be explored.

The archives of Istanbul are by far the most extensive in the Middle East. There are however others. Important regional collections exist in a number of Turkish provincial cities, with the aid of which useful work is being done in the hitherto somewhat neglected field of local history. In the former European provinces of the Ottoman Empire—especially in Hungary, Yugoslavia, and Bulgaria—important groups of documents were left behind by the departing Turks, and have been studied to good purpose by Orientalists in those countries. It is not impossible that similar collections of documents, in public or private possession, may yet come to light in the former Arab provinces of the Empire.

The modern states of the area are too new to have any very extensive archives to offer to the historian. Only in Egypt, where autonomous government is a century and a half old, is there a public record collection of major importance. The 'Abdin archives in Cairo contain rich documentation for the history of Egypt from the time of Muhammad 'Ali Pasha onwards.

Besides the archives in oriental countries, there are also smaller but better-known collections of oriental documents in many European centres. Treaties, letters, and other documents of Egyptian Mamluk provenance are to be found in a number of Italian and Spanish cities that once maintained diplomatic and commercial relations with the Mamluk Sultanate. Moroccan and Persian diplomatic documents are preserved in several European record offices, and, most important of all, Ottoman documents in great numbers are to be found all over Europe, in the archives of almost every state that had dealings with the Sublime Porte. It was with these that the scientific study of Ottoman diplomatic began.

To these two main groups, the chronicles and the documents, we should perhaps add a third. It has generally been the practice that with the beginning of large-scale European activity and influence in the lands of Islam from the beginning of the 19th century, the Orientalist withdraws from the field and leaves it to his colleague, the historian.

The European Orientalist, mainly concerned with classical Islam, has generally been uninterested in the period of its decay and in its progressive subjection to European influence. The European historian who is interested in this process generally knows no Arabic, Persian, or Turkish, and remains totally unaware of the whole inner life of the area. The recent and contemporary history of the Islamic world has been left chiefly to the colonial and diplomatic historian, to the economist and to the current affairs expert. Between them they have done extremely valuable work of research and exposition of modern Middle Eastern history—how valuable may be judged by the fact that most modern Middle Eastern historians have preferred to follow in their footsteps rather than strike out on independent lines of investigation which they should be well qualified to pursue. The whole picture resulting from their endeavours, however, remains external. It is unrelated to the vital inner movements and developments, the study of which is possible and necessary, but which can only be based on the extensive use of local sources. These are available in great quantity—documents, pamphlets, memoirs, general literature, and, perhaps most important of all, the periodical and daily press. It is generally conceded that the study of the modern French requires some knowledge of French language and writings. Why should the Arabs, Persians, or Turks be different? It is true that their languages are more difficult, but that is not really an adequate answer.

For a long time this purely external approach to modern oriental history could to some extent be justified by the absence or inaccessibility of oriental documents and the paucity or poverty of modern oriental historians. But now this argument is losing its force. The great archive collections of Istanbul and Cairo are in part open, and oriental historians are publishing texts and monographs of increasing weight. The vernacular press is more than a century old, and the new literatures of the Arabs, Persians, and Turks offer an indispensable source of information on the evolution of attitudes and ideas.

There thus remains much to be done. There are chronicles to be edited, translated, and subjected to textual and historical criticism. There are documents, especially in the Ottoman archives, to be published, or at least calendared. There are topics and persons, places, events, and institutions to be monographed, auxiliary sciences to be developed, manuals to be written. In many of these fields contributions of increasing value are being made by oriental scholars, who are taking up and applying some of the techniques evolved by European Orientalists in the past.

But there is still much to be done by Western scholarship that in present circumstances will only be done by Western scholars. One of the most valuable of these things is the integration of the history of Islam into the study of the general history of humanity. I cannot do better in concluding than to quote the following generous tribute to Western oriental scholarship broadcast from Cairo radio by the eminent Egyptian historian, Shafiq Ghorbal:

"Perhaps the most useful contributions made by Western Orientalists to Arabic and Islamic studies are their works on Islamic history. For in addition to their skilful use of Arabic sources and their mastery of methods of criticism, analysis and exposition, they present Islamic history as a fundamental and inseparable part of the history of humanity, influencing it and being influenced by it, and they study Islamic societies as human societies that have been and are subject to the vicissitudes of societies, with human virtues and human failings, human perfection and human imperfection."

Bibliographical Note

(a) SELECTIVE AND ANNOTATED BIBLIOGRAPHIES

The best introduction to the study of Islamic history, containing a critical survey of the sources, problems, and literature, is that of the late Jean Sauvaget. First published in Paris in 1943, it was reprinted with addenda by the author in 1946, and republished, after his death, in a new edition, recast and revised by Claude Cahen (1961). This in turn was translated into English, with further revisions and additions, under the auspices of the Near East Centre at the University of California, Los Angeles: *Jean Sauvaget's Introduction to the history of the Muslim East: a bibliographical guide, based on the second edition as recast by Claude Cahen* (University of California Press, 1965). This may be supplemented by the relevant sections in the American Historical Association's *Guide to historical literature* (New York, 1961), and by more specialized works such as Francesco Gabrieli, "Studi di Storia Musulmana, 1940–1950"

(*Rivista Storica Italiana*, LXII, 1950, pp. 99–111), V. Minorsky, "Les études historiques sur la Perse depuis 1935" (*Acta Orientalia*, XXI, 1951, pp. 108–123), and Bertold Spuler and Ludwig Forrer, *Der Vordere Orient in Islamischer Zeit* (Bern, 1954). Earlier bibliographies that are still of value will be found in Giuseppe Gabrieli, *Manuale di Bibliografia Musulmana* (Rome, 1916) and Gustav Pfannmüller, *Handbuch der Islam-Literatur* (Berlin and Leipzig, 1923). Classified and annotated bibliographies of current work are published in the *Middle East Journal* (bibliography of periodical literature), the *Revue des Études Islamiques* (Abstracta Islamica), and, more briefly, in other journals devoted to Islamic studies.

(*b*) COMPREHENSIVE BIBLIOGRAPHIES

The standard work is that of J. D. Pearson, *Index Islamicus 1906–1955* (Cambridge, W. Heffer and Sons, 1958), containing a classified and indexed bibliography of articles in periodicals and other collective publications relating to Islam. This has been followed by supplements covering 1956–1960 (Cambridge, 1962) and 1961–1965 (Cambridge, 1967).

(*c*) GENERAL WORKS ON ISLAMIC HISTORY

A comprehensive history of Islam, from its origins to the present day, is in the press, and will shortly be published as the *Cambridge History of Islam*. Shorter accounts of Islamic history and civilization will be found in the relevant sections of the *Handbuch der Orientalistik*, I, *Der nahe und mittlere Osten*, ed. B. Spuler (Leiden and Cologne, 1952–   ), English translation in progress (Leiden, 1960–   ); *Le civiltà dell'Oriente* (Rome, (1956–   ); and in the survey edited by Father F. M. Pareja, *Islamologïa* I–II (Madrid, 1952–1954); also available in Italian and French. Sections on the Islamic states and peoples will also be found in a number of general historical works, such as the *Cambridge Medieval History*, especially vol. IV/1: *Byzantium and its neighbours*, ed. Joan M. Hussey (Cambridge University Press, 1966); the *Cambridge Modern History* (chapters on the Ottoman Empire); the *Cambridge History of India*; *Historia Mundi*, vols. VI and VII; *Propyläen-Weltgeschichte*, especially vol. V (Berlin, 1963); *Storia Universale*, ed. E. Pontieri; *Histoire générale des civilisations*, especially vol. III, *Le moyen âge*, ed.

E. Perroy (Paris, 1955). There are also chapters on Islamic history in the *History of the Crusades*, editor-in-chief K. M. Setton (Philadelphia, 1955–).

(*d*) WORKS OF REFERENCE

The main work of reference in this field is the *Encyclopaedia of Islam*, first edition, four volumes and supplement, 1913–1948; second edition in progress, 1954–

BERNARD LEWIS

INDIA AND ITS
CULTURAL EMPIRE

FEW parts of Asia lie so isolated from the rest of the great Eurasian continent as India.* In the South-West and South-East the vast and deep stretches of the Indian Ocean guard its coasts, while on the North the high ranges of the Himālayas protect its frontiers. To the West the country is bounded by the Baluchistan mountains and the terrible Thar desert further inland, and in the East by the swamps and marshes of the Ganges delta and the difficult hill tracts of northern Burma. This line of defence with which nature has provided the sub-continent acted not only as a barrier against foreign invasions, but also prevented regular and easy intercourse between India and the rest of Asia. This isolation may have encouraged the growth of a civilisation which became typical for this part of the world, and which by some of its peculiarities is quite different from any other civilisation in Asia.

This Indian civilisation came into existence in the first millennium B.C. as a result of the intermingling of Aryan and pre-aryan cultures. After conquering the Indus Valley, with its in several respects unsurpassed standard of urban life, sometime between 1800 and 1500 B.C., the nomadic Aryans settled down in the North-West of India and thence gradually encroached in an eastwardly direction upon the pre-aryan population of North India until the whole of the Ganges Valley was occupied. This movement must have been completed during the first half of the first millennium B.C. The resulting political aryanisation of this part of the country took place simultaneously with a process in which various pre-aryan elements in the material, religious and social fields of life were absorbed by the Aryans. The interaction of these two forces, political and cultural, must have been a gradual

* Throughout this chapter this name is used in the geographical or cultural sense, and not in the political sense which it acquired in 1947.

35

process, stretching out over many centuries; but by the time the curtain rises on the historical period, round about the 7th century B.C., Indian culture as it then presents itself already shows many of its typical aspects in the religious and social spheres of life.

The spectacle before us is a society in which the class of priests has acquired a preponderant position, while the warriors claim second place. There is however, not the slightest doubt that the bulk of the population consisted of farmers, and that economically speaking North India in those days was essentially agricultural and self-sufficient. The average Indian was, and still is today, a village peasant. In this respect India has scarcely changed in 2500 years.

Politically, at this time the country consisted of a great many states, principalities, republics and clans. This political multiplicity, which seems to prevail throughout the major part of Indian history, has led a famous French scholar to exclaim : "L'Inde n'a pas d'histoire." This may sound somewhat exaggerated, but whether we take it to mean that India has no single history, or that history was not produced as a branch of learning, both interpretations seem equally incontestable, as we shall see further on. Political multiplicity is certainly characteristic of India's history, for it is only during a few short periods that all, or nearly all of the subcontinent was ruled by one person. The most brilliant of these periods was Aśoka's purely Indian rule (274/3—237 or 232) over the Mauryan empire which extended from the southern part of the Deccan right into Afghanistan. During the three other periods in which India was ruled from one capital only, unity was forced upon the country from outside by foreigners : the Delhi Sultanate under Sultan Alā-ud-dīn-Khiljī (1296–1316) and his immediate successors; the Mogul empire under Aurangzeb (1659–1707); and finally the British rule. On the whole, however, these short periods of unity may be taken as exceptions. To regard this peculiarity of Indian history as a result of weakness, or as evidence of a lack of great men, is unjustified. India's vastness and its geographical conditions which even until recent times made travel difficult and dangerous, account to a great extent for its disrupted political history; this in its turn seems to have resulted in an absence of any strong national feeling. India's unity lay not so much in the political, as in the cultural sphere, in which Hinduism as a socio-religious system united the country in a way which was quite different from any political unity, and transcended its limitations. Nationalism, as such, has only sprung up in the last hundred years as a result of, and a reaction to, Western influences. Political unity was brought to India only through the British Rāj, and even that strong force was eventually not able to keep the whole subcontinent together.

In general, therefore, India was politically disrupted into many different kingdoms and this seems to be one of the main reasons for the remarkable fact that it did not play an important political rôle outside its frontiers. There was ample scope within the country for ambitious men seeking fame on the battle-field and consequently any display of military power across the borders was extremely rare. One such expedition was undertaken during the Cola period in South India. Not only was most of Ceylon occupied for a very long period, but also the Cola ruler sent a maritime force to the empire of Śrīvijaya in Sumatra and Malaya which captured the king and occupied the greater part of this South-East Asian maritime state. The political effect of this expedition does not seem to have been very great, however, nor to have lasted more than a few years.

Another reason why India's political influence did not extend beyond her frontiers was that in early times the country was self-sufficient, and consequently there was no cause—such as overpopulation—for expansion on economic grounds. While most countries in Asia had an intermittent political influence on one another, India's interests remained almost exclusively domestic.

However politically disunited India may have been, culturally it was to achieve a fine unity after the Indo-Aryan civilisation of the North had gradually spread across the southern part of the country during the second half of the first millennium B.C. It seems as if Indo-Aryan culture was readily acceptable to the South, perhaps because with its pre-aryan substratum it had already several elements in common with the Dravidian culture. Here, in South India, history once more proves the rule that converts are more orthodox than the original exponents of a culture or religion, for the Dravidian country became the very bulwark of Hinduism in the days of Muslim paramountcy.

*　　*　　*

It would be impossible to describe Indian civilisation adequately in a few lines, and this is not in fact the purpose of this chapter. But it should be stressed that the greatest accomplishments lie in the cultural sphere. India's religions and philosophical systems have been acknowledged as some of the finest achievements of the human mind; and it is well to remember that India is the cradle of the oldest extant world religion. In the field of literature many different types were developed : epic, drama, novels, fables, etc. An extensive religious literature of the early period has come down to us, the bulk of which was transmitted orally in order to preserve the secret priestly knowledge from unworthy prying eyes. This is why script was introduced relatively late. From the 4th to 3rd centuries B.C. onwards we find two scripts in use : Kharoṣṭhī in the North-West and Brāhmī in the rest of the country. In the 5th century A.D., Kharoṣṭhī disappears, and hence forth Brāhmī in its many regional developments reigns supreme, eventually even becoming the ancestor of several Central Asian and all the numerous South and South-East Asian scripts. Indian culture reached a high level in grammar, law, political theory, architecture, sculpture, painting and music, while a remarkable degree of skill was achieved in such arts and crafts as metal casting, enamel work and jewelry, ivory and wood carving. In the various branches of science, on the other hand, Indian genius is not so immediately apparent, but medicine, mathematics, and astronomy attained a high degree of development, while such technical wonders as the iron pillar at Delhi, baffling even modern scientists, witness to the fact that chemistry and metallurgy had also achieved a remarkable standard. Finally, special mention should be made of the fact that it was almost certainly in

India that that most ingenious system of calculation based on nine digits and zero was invented, a world discovery of the first rank.

The remarkable thing about all these achievements in the arts and sciences is that they are practically wholly based on the religions and philosophies of the culture which produced them, something of which modern Western research in both branches can hardly boast. Thus religion, art, and science worked together in beneficial harmony, promoting and stimulating one another's potentialities. This religiously inspired creative genius started to work far back in proto-historic times, and except in science, is active to this day.

*   *   *

Having surveyed Indian culture very briefly, we can now assess its relations with foreign cultures. As we have seen, the country was provided with natural frontiers which warded off foreign intrusion to a considerable extent. There were, however, a few passes in the North-West and in Baluchistan, such as the Hindu Kush and the Bolan Pass; and at several times in history these gateways to India have been forced, with a resultant influx of foreign people and their alien culture into the northern plains. Undoubtedly the fame of India's riches had long reached these tribes of Mongol or Aryan stock living on the North-East and North-West frontiers, and when an·opportunity in the form of weak rulers or internecine wars presented itself, they eagerly grasped it. Politically, the history of North India was often dictated by the incursions of the barbarian foreigners, but Indian civilisation proved to be so superior to the culture of the newcomers, that it was not endangered by the foreign elements so introduced. On the contrary, after a lapse of time those elements which fitted into the pattern of Indian culture were gradually incorporated, thus enriching Indian civilisation, and the rest were discarded. The invaders for their part were gradually amalgamated physically with the original population, and sooner or later they adopted Indian culture in its various aspects. In early Indian history they were often indeed assimilated to such an extent that they became part of the socio-religious system of

Hinduism by forming a new caste, thus becoming Hindus, something that was theoretically impossible. Without exception the victors were eventually themselves vanquished.

In more recent times, however, Indian civilisation has twice had to face a foreign culture which seemed to endanger its existence : the Muslim culture, and that of Western Europe. In both cases Indian civilisation reacted to the assault in much the same way, by retiring into the fortress of its strong tradition, and by throwing up a rampart of conservatism. The forces which lie hidden in this passive but traditional background should not be underestimated. Foreign elements are simply not allowed to enter Hindu family life, the basic unit of the great socio-religious system which keeps Indian civilisation together. Foreigners are ostracised and are forced to form a new group among themselves, thus becoming segregated in the midst of hostile surroundings, the third possibility, apart from absorption or rejection, when two cultures meet. The impact of Islam upon India has certainly left its traces, but, because the Muslim community was never socially or religiously absorbed by the Indian, these traces are largely confined to the material culture which, from the Indian point of view, is not so important. Cultural influences through the means of Sufis and Bhaktis were indeed distinct, but never produced considerable changes. On the rare occasions when they influenced Indian thought they seem only to have enriched it. Muslim influence was generally restricted to the urban areas, except in East Bengal and the North-West, and consequently the life of the average Indian, the village peasant, did not show any considerable change.

Western civilisation, however, embodied mainly in the British rule, brought about numerous changes in the sub-continent, not only in the material sphere—and that to a far greater extent than the impact of Islam—but also in the socio-religious sphere. The stronghold of Indian civilisation, its community life, based on traditions of religion and culture, was severely undermined. In certain urban areas this traditional background has even started to disintegrate, and the younger generation of intellectuals and semi-intellectuals often seems to have lost touch with it, unintentionally or deliberately breaking away from it. Whether it will be possible to stop this process remains to be seen. The period of Western impact has not ended with the withdrawal of the British from Indian soil. Undoubtedly Indian civilisation will more easily be able to protect itself from the impact, now that it feels itself sustained by the ideal and the accomplished fact of independence. It will be interesting to observe to what extent the ancient Indian genius of absorption is still alive, adopting into its cultural pattern those elements which do not disturb it too much, and discarding others as valueless. Taking the events of the past as a parallel one would be inclined to believe that Indian culture will survive, be it after a period of acute ferment.

Just as the natural frontiers did not eventually prevent foreigners from intruding into India, so they did not altogether prevent Indians from leaving their country; but there seems to have been no large-scale emigration except in recent times. This can probably be largely attributed to two factors already mentioned : India's lack of sufficient military prestige to back emigration; and her economic self-sufficiency, indeed, we might say economic and cultural self-sufficiency, for to the Indian everything outside the pale of his civilisation was barbaric and to be shunned. Why should he leave the safe and well-known shores and plains of India, where he had his appointed place in an age-old social pattern ? The reluctance to travel abroad is reflected in the taboo against Brahmins' crossing the sea. Ancient Indian literature contains many stories about dangers encountered by those who ventured outside India, but there is little or no mention of Indians settling definitely abroad. Those who did visit foreign countries were either merchants lured by profit, or religious men urged by faith. Bearing in mind that India's geographical and social environment threw up barriers against emigration for all but the very few courageous individualists, we may be all the more surprised that Indian influence spread so widely. However, the history of Indian expansion is not that of colonisation in the sense of political domination and settlement, but of colonisation in the cultural sense, and India's sphere of influence extended itself in this way until it embraced large areas of Asia.

The first cultural ambassadors we know of are the missionaries sent abroad by the Emperor Aśoka to spread the knowledge of Buddhism. In edict no. XIII (one of the rock inscriptions found engraved all over India, as far apart as Shāhbāzgarhī in the North-West, and Dhaulī on the east coast, or Maski in the Dravidian South) this remarkable ruler tells us that he sent these emissaries to the courts of several Hellenistic kings, who have been identified as Antiochus II Theos of Syria, Ptolemy II Philadelphus of Egypt, Antigonus Gonatas of Macedonia, Magas of Cyrene, and Alexander of Epirus. Such emissaries were also sent to all the neighbouring peoples such as the Colas and Pāṇḍyas in the South, or the Greeks and Kambojas in the North-West. The result of the missions to the Hellenistic West do not seem to have been very great, but those sent to the North-West, to the South and to Ceylon were of great consequence and resulted ultimately in the spread of Buddhism and Indian culture throughout India. Buddhism, with its democratic character embodied in its scorn for caste-system and priest-rule, was more acceptable to foreigners than Hinduism, and this partly explains its success in converting the frontier people. Not only did Buddhism influence the "barbarians", it was itself in turn influenced by them, so that foreign elements crept into the Buddhist creed, changing it from a typically Indian into a more universal religion. Its democratic principles and this subsequently acquired flexibility made Buddhism potentially a world religion, as it in fact became after conquering the greater part of Asia.

In this connection it is interesting to note the contrast between Buddhism and Jainism. Both religions came into existence at about the same time, they were both the outcome of religious ferment in the 6th century B.C. in India, and in fact their creed and worship were in many respects similar. In the last few centuries B.C., however, Buddhism came into contact, through Aśoka's zeal, with the peoples on the fringes of Indian civilisation, and as a result it became more catholic. Jainism, on the other hand, remained within the sphere of pure Indian culture, and in its struggle to maintain itself against the influence of surrounding Hinduism became increasingly orthodox, thereby emphasising its Indian features, and reducing the chances of its being acceptable to foreigners. Consequently the development of the two creeds reduced their resemblance, the one expanding ever more widely, the other becoming more and more exclusively Indian.

Towards the beginning of the Christian era the whole of India and Ceylon had become thoroughly Aryanised. A large part of the credit for this achievement probably goes to Buddhism. Concerning Ceylon, tradition holds that the Emperor Aśoka's own son led the group of missionaries sent to the island to convert the Singhalese king and his people, which seems credible in the light of Aśoka's own rock inscriptions. Whether the conversion went as smoothly as tradition would have us believe is another matter; but in any case, once converted, Ceylon has remained true to Buddhism up to this day, whereas Buddhism has, except in the Himālayas and in a few small places here and there, virtually vanished from Indian soil.

Buddhism was as successful in the North-West of India as in Ceylon, although there it has not survived. Gandhāra, as this region was called in ancient days, became a seat of Buddhism second only to Magadha, its birthplace. Many monasteries and places of pilgrimage dotted the country, and so holy was its reputation, that not a few Chinese pilgrims who undertook the dangerous journey to India to visit the sacred places of Buddhism, considered their efforts rewarded once they had reached Gandhāra.

The triumphal spread of Indian culture did not halt at the natural frontiers of the country. In the North-West it crossed the mountain passes and penetrated into Afghanistan and thence into Central Asia. From there it travelled on along the ancient trade-routes through present-day Chinese Turkestan, which linked China with the West and eventually reached the western frontiers of China. Next to trade, Buddhism seems throughout to have been the main vehicle of Indian influence. After reaching the Chinese borders Buddhism even gained entrance to China itself, bearing with it various material forms of Indian culture which it used as its media of expression : literature, sculpture, painting, and so on. Through China, Buddhism finally passed on into Korea and

Japan. During this vast journey several foreign elements crept in, and Buddhism as well as Buddhist art and literature became often to some degree adapted to the culture of their new environment.

In later times, somewhere in the 7th century A.D., Buddhism once more broke through the mountains in the North and penetrated into that wild and until then still practically uncivilised country, Tibet. After a severe struggle the country was converted, and has remained ever since a stronghold of that evolved type of Buddhism popularly known as Lamaism. Again Indian culture followed in the wake of Buddhism and a considerable amount of Tibetan culture can be said to be of Indian stock. In its turn Tibet converted the mighty Chinese dynasty of the Yüan, of Mongol extraction, which then whole-heartedly supported a Buddhist campaign to convert Mongolia.

Nor was Indian culture restricted by natural barriers in the South. It crossed the ocean to reach South-East Asia in the first few centuries of the Christian era and as a result mixed cultures with Indian characteristics sprang up in several places. These new cultures were widely divergent because of the dissimilarity between the indigenous roots on which the Indian strains were grafted. In many cases the natives had already reached a certain stage of development before the Indian influences made themselves felt so that such arts and crafts as weaving, dyeing, and carving had often already acquired a form typical of their locality. Moreover, several areas had also acquired knowledge of such subjects as wet rice-cultivation, astronomy, and metallurgy, so that there is less traceable evidence of Indian influence in these subjects. The new mixed cultures of South-East Asia were certainly not just reproductions of Indian civilisation. They were something altogether new, the result of the fertilisation of basic cultures by the riches of Indian achievement, generally of a higher cultural order, in such spheres as script, literature, grammar, religion, philosophy, mythology, political theory, law, architecture, sculpture, and different branches of science.

Unlike the cultural expansion to Central and East Asia, this south-eastern expansion was not predominantly due to

Buddhism. Hinduism too, in all its forms—though mostly Śivaitic—enjoyed several periods of popularity in many areas, and in its tantric development it greatly influenced Buddhism, not only inside India, but abroad, in South-East Asia. However, the very first traces of Indian influences in some south-eastern countries are Buddhistic, which bears out the assumption that the first contacts were probably made with the then predominantly Buddhist east coast of India. Similarly, the important part played by Hinduism in South-East Asia in subsequent times can be accounted for by the fact that the east coast later became Hindu.

There are reasons for believing that the first contacts between India and South-East Asia took place in the 1st century A.D., contacts which were almost certainly mercantile. Judging by the fairly detailed account of the geography of this part of Asia which Ptolemy was able to give, this trade must have increased in the 2nd century A.D. What could have been the reason for this trade, and why did it start in the 1st century and then expand so rapidly ? Although contact between India and the Mediterranean goes back to protohistoric times, it remained indirect until about 100 B.C.,[1] when Hippalus discovered the secret of the monsoon winds, closely guarded by the Arab traders to protect their monopoly as middlemen.

With the establishment of the Roman empire a trade-boom started, for Rome, now wealthy as a result of the Pax Romana, could afford to indulge in the commodities offered by the East. Thus a bustling trade grew up in a great many oriental luxuries such as spices, pearls and ivory. Some of this merchandise came from farther East than India, for example tortoise-shell, the finest of which, as Ptolemy specifically noted, came from South-East Asia. I submit that it was this demand in the Roman West for South-East Asian wares which gave the original impetus to the improvement in communications between the coasts of South-East India and South-East Asia in the 1st and 2nd centuries A.D. There are indications that from then on there was regular intercourse, although

[1] The arguments for this early date are given in *Eudoxus van Cyzicus*, by J. H. Thiel. Med. Kon. Akad., Afd. Lett. N.R., Vol. 2, No. 8, Amsterdam, 1939.

occasional voyages may have been made to those parts of Asia before. The merchants and sailors on the south and east coasts of India were geographically best situated to carry on this trade with the South-East, and it is exactly in these parts of India that we find important Roman emporia, where the traders from the West could exchange their wares with those produced by India, and at the same time meet the Indian merchants returning with coveted wares from their journeys to South-East Asia. Once trade had been established between India and the South-East, the relations continued and intensified not for mercantile, but for cultural reasons. For as soon as the peoples of South-East Asia had realised the benefits of Indian culture, with its tremendous store of artistic and scientific achievement, they were eager to learn more about it. In the wake of Indian merchants followed the bearers of civilisation, learned priests and monks, either on their own initiative, or, as is more probable, at the request of the rulers of the first Indianised kingdoms. Traffic however, was not in one direction only; for India's fame as a home of learning soon attracted a stream of pilgrims from the South-East as well as from the Far East. After spending some years in the different centres of learning they returned to their own countries taking new knowledge and inspiration with them. The Indianisation effected by these scholars should not be under-estimated, and there is reason to believe that it may well have been more important than the influence of the relatively few Indians who settled in South-East Asia. The strength of the influence of India in cultural matters is best illustrated by the fact that some of the greatest surviving architectural creations in the Indian world, for example Barabudur and Lara Jong-grang in Java, and Angkor Vat in Cambodia, were conceived and erected in South-East Asia.

It should, however, be remembered that each of the various mixed cultures which sprang up in this area centred on the king and his court. The higher strata of the population, the nobles and intellectuals, including some of the religious men, all followed court fashions, and it is this group which must be considered as the bearers of the new mixed cultures. So, the further away from the court, geographically as well as socially, the stronger the indigenous elements in the mixed cultures. Thus in the early centuries of the Christian era petty Indianised kingdoms sprang up in different parts of South-East Asia, such as the present day Burma, Thailand, Malaya, Indonesia and Indo-China. Some of these kingdoms developed into important realms and even empires, others were soon overrun by the political expansion of mightier neighbours.

In the kingdom of Campā, on the east coast of Indo-China, Indian culture reached its farthest limit on the South Asian mainland; beyond this country to the North lay the empire of Annam, which had been thoroughly influenced by China at a very early period.

Unlike the meeting in Central Asia of India and China, the contact of these two great civilisations in Indo-China created friction and Campā's history is a story of continual struggle against the oncoming tide of the Annamite armies, to which Campā, after heroic efforts finally gave way in the 15th century.

Indian culture was also eclipsed in Indonesia, though not as completely as in Campā. In the beginning of the 16th century Islam peacefully conquered and converted the main centres in the Indian Archipelago with the exception of Bali where an Indo-Balinese civilisation still flourishes. Many elements of the previous Indo-Javanese period were incorporated in the new Javanese culture, however, and in fact at first only a few superficial modifications seem to have been made. It is only in the last hundred years, with the sudden vast improvements in travel, that the ancient Indo-Javanese elements have gradually been discarded or replaced by more orthodox Muslim ideas, as a result of the increasing intercourse with the home country of Islam.

Ceylon, Burma, Thailand and the western and southern part of Indo-China still continue to form part of the Indian cultural sphere, although the eighteen odd centuries that have passed since the first spread of Indian culture have witnessed considerable changes in each area, as a result of the penetration of foreign influence and the reassertion of original, indigenous elements.

After this survey of India's influence in the North, North-East, South and South-East, only the expansion to the West

remains for consideration. In the last centuries B.C. Afghanistan was converted to Buddhism, and several parts of Iran
were affected by it. A Chinese source even mentions the
name of an Arsacidian prince who became a monk and
preached Buddhism in China. But Buddhism in its turn was
also influenced, and some of the Iranian elements in it date
from this period. Still further westwards Indian philosophy
had already gained respect and fame, so much so that men like
Apollonius of Tyana and Plotinus were eager to visit the
country in order to obtain first hand information.

In general the contacts between India and the West are
more conspicuous on the material plane. Many commodities
were traded to the Mediterranean from early times, and under
the Roman empire this trade became of great importance.
After the rise of Islam to power in the Near East, the Arab
world became the channel between India and the West, and
many elements of Indian culture passed through the Muslim
states to Europe. Mathematics, astronomy, and medicine,
particularly appealed to the Muslims, and it is to this fact
that we owe our use of the system of nine digits with place
value, the conception of zero, and the game of chess. As
early as the 6th century B.C. literary motifs of Indian origin
found their way into the Near East. We can even trace the
routes which some of the stories followed later via translations
into Pahlavi, Arabic, Persian, Syriac, Latin, Hebrew, Spanish
and other European languages. During one such transmission a most astonishing metamorphosis occurred whereby
the Bodhisattva, the future Buddha, became a Christian saint
called Josaphat. Apart from literature, the influence of
Indian arts on Muslim and Christian culture in the West is
not so significant. The civilisations of both religions had their
own specific requirements and needed little or nothing from
India in this way, particularly since Greek and Roman culture
had amply provided for their needs. Consequently cultural
expansion towards the West was weaker than in other
directions. Apart from some stray influences such as those
exercised by Indian paintings on the works of Rembrandt,
Western Europe was little affected by India until the end of
the 18th century, when its ancient civilisation was discovered

by West European scholars. The translations of Indian literary and philosophical texts which resulted from this discovery were a revelation to great European writers such as Goethe and Schopenhauer, and they have continued to influence the West ever since.

*   *   *

Reviewing the extent of the empire of Indian culture, we have seen that in time its inception still lies concealed in the haze of protohistory, sometime about the end of the second millennium or the beginning of the first millennium B.C., and that it continues to exist to this day. In space, its frontiers have moved forwards and backwards in the course of the ages, at one time embracing the whole of Central, South and South-East Asia, while the Far East and the Muslim world might in several respects be termed importers of Indian culture. In the course of this expansion India scarcely ever forced her culture upon any area, partly because she had not sufficient military and political power, and partly perhaps because of the Indian's inherent and deep-rooted aversion to violence, expressed throughout his philosophy and religions. This aversion is such an important factor in the Indian's outlook on life that we should not overlook the possibility that it actually played some part in the moulding of Indian history. But, wherever the cause is to be found—on the material or the spiritual plane—it is clear that the cultural empire India built for herself was built by peaceful means.

*   *   *

The student of Indian history, as of any other history, is dependent on the literary and non-literary sources inside India and abroad; but here an exceptionally high proportion of his information will be derived from foreign sources, since a feature of Indian culture is the almost complete absence of historical literature in the modern sense. In this respect India stands in striking contrast to China, for example. The fact that India, in spite of her great intellectual achievements, did not produce historical writings calls for some explanation. Chronicles were indeed made at several courts, but most of them have now been lost, the reason being that from the Indian point of view factual information about a particular dynasty was, in comparison to spiritual issues, of little interest except to the descendants of that dynasty. History was important to the average Indian only for the light which it could throw on the perennial truths of the Hindu philosophy and as a record of exemplary lives. It follows that, as a rule, only those parts of history were preserved in Indian literature which contained these prerequisites. From the point of view of a modern historian India's historical tradition is therefore often badly mutilated; but we must not forget that the Indian writer never aimed at recording history. His main goal was to create a piece of aesthetic literature dealing with Indian ideals in life. Historical accuracy was an entirely secondary consideration, which would be jettisoned for the sake of the main purpose. Consequently history, myth, legend, and imagination flow into one, and it is left to the present-day historian to try to unravel historical facts from the entangled mass of Indian literature. Accuracy was further obscured by the tendency to hand down texts by word of mouth. During this process accounts which had little magical significance, such as chronicles, were the most subject to change.

One class of Indian literature, the Purāṇas, deserves special mention, because in part these texts approximate closely to chronicles and dynastic lists from which almost certainly the nucleus of most of them was derived. In the form of prophecies they give the history of the world from the creation onwards, forecasting the dynasties which will rule India in the time to come. Facts and figures given by these Purāṇas may sometimes be of help to the historian, but they should be used with the utmost caution. There was a time when historians entirely rejected the material in the Purāṇas as unreliable, but it seems that by the advancement of other branches of learning such as archaeology, numismatics, palaeography, and epigraphy, some statements in the Purāṇas may be corroborated and provide useful additional material.

Only one Sanskrit work qualifies as real history, the *Rājataraṅgiṇī*, a history of Kashmir written by the poet Kalhaṇa. By virtue of his birth as the son of a former minister, the author knew and saw much of what went on at the court of Kashmir. The fact that he himself did not participate in politics, but held aloof from all intrigues, made him an independent observer of the turbulent events of his time—the 12th century. His critical methods of using, comparing and weighing many different sources show his historical attitude of mind, and apart from the first four chapters on early Kashmirian history, the *Rājataraṅginī* ranks as a really fine work. Kalhaṇa's example shows that India did produce minds able to carry out historical research; but the general attitude towards history encouraged every promising young man of letters to concentrate his abilities on other branches of learning, which offered greater rewards to those seeking fame.

The languages in which the Indian sources are written range throughout the length and breadth of the subcontinent and right through the centuries, from the Vedic Sanskrit of the Aryan invaders down to the modern Indian vernaculars. A substantial part is written in classical Sanskrit, but the amount in Prakrits (Middle Indian vernaculars out of which the modern Indian languages developed) should not be underestimated. Buddhists and Jainas used these Prakrits for their literature, which contains no small quantity of historical information when carefully sifted. In the Dravidian South sources are written in one or other of the Dravidian languages or again in Sanskrit. Some of the early sources which might be used for the reconstruction of Indian history no longer exist on Indian soil and in an Indian language, but have fortunately been preserved for us in a Central Asian, Chinese or Tibetan translation.

Many sources concerning the period after the Muslim invasion are in Persian or in Urdu, a vernacular which came into being in the North as a result of the mixture of Persian and Hindustani. Then from the 16th century onwards, contact with the European seafaring nations produced records in Portuguese, Dutch, French, Danish and English. Though some of the later sources are Indian, the majority of them are of foreign origin.

The earliest foreign sources bearing on Indian history are some Persian inscriptions dating from the late 6th century B.C.

Soon after that the classical sources become of value, Alexander's campaign in India greatly stimulating the Western authors to increase their knowledge of that fabulous country. Thereafter, during the Roman period, there was regular contact between the two great civilisations. Later on, after the fall of the Roman empire and the rise of Islam, intercourse with the Mediterranean was practically cut off; but the work of the classical authors was continued by Arabs and Persians, some scholars, and some merchants who had travelled to India. In many cases their works contain invaluable information, because feeling for history was so much stronger in the Muslim world than in India.

Not only to the West, but also to the East of India, in China, there is an important fund of information for its history. Few peoples are able to boast of a finer historical tradition than the Chinese. Their painstaking records of the foreign peoples living near their borders, or even further away, illuminated with historical notes added by the scribes from time to time about these particular areas, are often of help to the historian dealing with India. In the case of South-East Asian history the help of the Chinese records is quite indispensable and they are often the only source available for a certain period.

Apart from the works in Chinese, such as the Annals or travel accounts by pilgrims, which can be useful as sources for Indian history, there is also a considerable number of works, mostly Buddhist, which were translated from the original Indian languages into Chinese and which in some cases contain information otherwise destroyed and lost in India. The same applies to some works translated into Central Asian languages and Tibetan. Tibet, being a near neighbour, has also furnished us with some original texts with bearings on Indian history, such as Tāranātha's "History of Buddhism in India."

Concerning the literary sources, it will be seen that up to about the 13th century, when Muslim authors in India begin to provide more abundant data, the foreign sources are comparatively of far greater importance than in most other areas of Asia, because by virtue of their nature the indigenous sources are relatively speaking poor.

What, though, of the other sources available for reconstructing India's past? Here archaeology, with its various branches offers the most fertile field of research, correspondingly more important than in many other parts of Asia, since India's literary sources are so unproductive. The most striking example of the importance of archaeology was the discovery of the Harappa civilisation in the Indus Valley, whereby Indian protohistory was extended overnight from the middle of the first millennium B.C. back to the middle of the third millennium; and the latest discoveries in Baluchistan have proved the existence of settlements as early as ±3100 B.C. It is indeed the archaeology of the spade which has yielded practically everything we know about the history of man in the Indian subcontinent from the Middle Pleistocene age down to the middle of the second millennium B.C., the point at which the oldest parts of the Vedas start to throw some dim light on the earliest Aryan settlements in North-West India. Linguistics have been of some help in reconstructing the movements of peoples in pre- and protohistorical times, but even so, we are likely to have to depend on archaeology to reveal more clearly what happened in the centuries down to about the middle of the first millennium B.C.—when for the first time the curtain rises on Indian civilisation—for the available literary sources are quite inadequate for the reconstruction of the historical events, and linguistics can only supply some broad outlines.

From the 7th or 6th century B.C. onwards archaeology and literature become complementary, and supplement one another to produce invaluable evidence; it is here that such branches of archaeology as numismatics, iconography, epigraphy, and palaeography come to the fore. Sometimes, as in the case of the Hellenistic rulers of North-West India, the historian has to rely practically entirely on numismatics, and in many periods epigraphy is the only available source. Fortunately there is abundant material in these branches of archaeology, but there are factors which render this type of research hazardous and far from straight-forward; for instance, the use throughout the country of many different, frequently unspecified eras in the dating of inscriptions; or the fact that coins often continued to circulate centuries after they were minted.

At the end of the 18th century India's rich cultural heritage was discovered by Western Europe. It was the labour of Western scholars which for the first time produced a history of India in the modern sense, and which drew India's attention to her own cultural past. During the 19th century Indian scholars began to share in this field of research, and East and West now both make contributions.

From the foregoing it will be apparent that the ideal student of Indian history would have to exhibit a staggering array of accomplishments, for apart from a grounding in historical methods and approach, he must be able to consult his sources. So in addition to familiarity with practically all the Indian languages, Indo-Aryan as well as Dravidian in all the stages of their development, he would have to command a knowledge of Latin, Greek, Arabic, Persian, Chinese, Portuguese, Dutch, Danish, French and English, and, as a result of research done in the 19th and 20th century, German and other languages. This is not all. For his studies of the early and mediaeval periods he would have to be an archaeologist, an epigraphist and a numismatist, and in order to be able to interprete his material he should have a sound knowledge of Indian religions, customs, manners, and so on. Obviously no single person can ever aspire to master all these branches of learning. The above enumeration simply serves to stress the multiplicity and diversity in time as well as in space of the available sources for Indian history. The prescription for avoiding mental indigestion is to get one's teeth into a small fragment rather than to attempt the impossible by nibbling at the whole mass. Specialisation in a period prior to the 13th century requires a sound knowledge of Sanskrit and the Prakrit or vernacular of one's special area and period, as well as a solid background of the different branches of archaeology. Some good grounding in the knowledge of the anthropological, religious, and social aspects of Indian culture would also be advisable. Those who would specialise rather in a period after the 13th century need a knowledge of Persian, and in addition the languages of some of the former colonial powers in India.

For both categories a working knowledge of those European languages in which the most important publications on Indian history have appeared is indispensable.

How far then can the general historian venture into this dense jungle of histories, general, regional, and local? The great obstacle here is that many sources are not yet available in translation, although quite a number of works have been translated, and many inscriptions can be found in translation in such series as *Epigraphia Indica, Epigraphia Zeylanica, Epigraphia Indo-Moslemica*, or the *Corpus Inscriptionum Indicarum*; but a great deal more work will have to be done before it will be possible to carry out research in early and mediaeval Indian history without the help of the specialist's knowledge of epigraphy or languages for instance—and it is extremely doubtful whether such research would ever be possible without that specialised training, or could achieve anything more than the questionable gain of knowledge compiled at second-hand. Post-13th-century Indian history, however, does not demand such specialised training, and here the general historian is confronted with far fewer pitfalls and difficulties.

There is one great danger which all students of Indian history should guard against: the interpretation of the facts as revealed by the sources in terms of one's personal environment, beliefs, and attitude to life. Every historian must be wary of this, but none more than those studying the history of a civilisation so complex and bewildering as that of India, with its many intricate social and psychological prescriptions and barriers. Here, if anywhere, the historian should try to see the facts in their own environment, and also at times through the eyes of those who took part in the events and were the bearers of the culture he is studying. This clearly is at times an extremely difficult task, but it has to be aimed at continually; and it is precisely for this reason that the student of Indian history should have a knowledge of Indian religions and society in its various aspects. Only by trying to place himself in the Indian society in which the historical events took place can the historian hope to grasp something of the background of these events and what caused them. He should however, endeavour to remain an objective judge, although the very fact that he tries to identify himself with the object and the cultural background of his research robs him to some extent of his impartiality. The struggle to follow these two ways of approach at the same time seems inevitable, although some may not clearly realise the existence of this duality in their approach, while others may deliberately choose one way only. It is in this respect that the personality of the historian for better or for worse, plays a part in his researches.

As for the future prospects of research, in practically every period there is ample scope for advance. There may seem less to be done in the early period than in the mediaeval, because the available sources are not so profuse and most of them have already been investigated. In mediaeval history the materials are rich. Inscriptions are numerous and so are the branches of regional and local history. With the advent of the Moguls and the Europeans the picture of India's history becomes clearer because there are more literary sources available. Moreover, these are more easily accessible to Western scholars, and consequently have been studied more fully.

*   *   *

In one way the South of Asia influenced world history greatly without intending to do so. It began in the sphere of commerce, with luxuries being sent to the Roman West as far back as the first centuries of the Christian era or even earlier. The demand for these oriental commodities grew, and the blockade of the normal trade-routes by the growing Muslim power in the Middle and Near East finally forced the Portuguese to search for new routes. After the rounding of the Cape of Good Hope, the new ocean highway to the riches of the Indian world was discovered, and not long afterwards other European nations followed along the same route. Spices were the most sought-for merchandise and to this day many Indian names of spices continue to be used in several European languages, though the incorporation of some of them as far back as the Roman period has long since obscured their origin. The peppercorn was even the cause, one might say, why large tracts of the strange Orient were unveiled to the wondering eyes of Europe, indeed, the discovery of the whole world resulted from the trading of such diminutive culinary delicacies, for without the search for the East, the New World would not have been found in the way it was. Rightly might the resultant influence of India on the world be called undesigned, for who could have foreseen the fruits which the pepperseed would bear when brought to the West: the entire change-over of political power in the East and in the whole world, in which the West went to the East to trade, to conquer and to rule; and it is only in our own day that the last chapter of this commercial and political enterprise of the West is being shaped and written.

Apart from this unintentional though very significant influence on events in the West, India did not greatly contribute to the shaping of European history. In Asia her influence was all the stronger; an influence almost exclusively cultural, with its greatest achievements in the realm of philosophical and religious thought together with considerable contributions to the various branches of the arts, and, to a lesser extent, the sciences, the first mainly to the North, South and East, and the second to the countries westward. The striking peculiarity of Indian history is that—with extraordinary conformity to the general Indian attitude to life in which facts as such do not matter—it is a history, not of a dominion of the sword, but of an Empire of the idea.

Bibliographical Note

SOUTH AND SOUTHEAST ASIA

C. H. Philips (editor), *Handbook of Oriental History* (Reprint: London, Offices of the Royal Historical Society, 1963). Contains select glossaries, lists of dynasties and rulers, and useful information on the romanization of words, on names and titles, and on systems of dating.

R. R. Sellman, *An Outline Atlas of Eastern History* (London, Edward Arnold, 1954). Fifty-three clear maps illustrating the geography and historical development of the various regions of Asia.

D. Seckel, *Kunst des Buddhismus, Werden Wanderung und Wandlung* (Baden-Baden, Holle Verlag, Kunst der Welt, 1964). English edition *The Art of Buddhism*, translated by A. E. Keep (London, Methuen, Art of the World Series, 1964). A survey of Buddhist art with almost 100 pictures, of which some 60 are in colour, and 73 instructive line-blocks, including many architectural plans.

R. E. M. Wheeler (editor), *Splendours of the East; Temples, Tombs, Palaces and Fortresses of Asia* (London, Weidenfeld and Nicolson, 1965). A picture book with short introductions on select sites, lavishly illustrated in colour and black and white.

P. Thomas, *Hindu Religion, Customs and Manners, Describing the Customs and Manners, Religious, Social and Domestic Life, Arts and Sciences of the Hindus*, 3rd Indian edition (Bombay, Taraporevala Sons & Co., 1956). With 260 illustrations.

E. Zürcher, *Buddhism, Its Origin and Spread in Words, Maps and Pictures* (Amsterdam, Djambatan, 1962). A concise history of Buddhism, its doctrines, organization, and main schools, and its spread into the various countries clearly illustrated by 11 maps.

India

C. H. Philips (editor), *Historians of India, Pakistan and Ceylon* (Oxford University Press, 1961). Thirty-five contributions by various experts on Indian historiography.

R. C. Majumdar (editor), *The History and Culture of the Indian People*, I–X (Bombay, Bharatiya Vidya Bhavan, 1951–). A scholarly and detailed history of ancient, medieval, and modern India of which several parts are still to appear. Some of the volumes contain extensive chapters on the various aspects of society and culture. Each chapter, to which a long and detailed bibliography is added, is written by a specialist in the field.

The Cambridge History of India I–VI (Indian reprint of the Cambridge Press edition: Delhi, S. Chand & Co., 1955–1958). An extensive political history of India before 1947 by various authors. Vol. II is still to be published.

J. Allan, *The Cambridge Shorter History of India* (Indian reprint of the Cambridge University Press edition: Delhi, S. Chand & Co., 1958). A summary of the previous item.

A History of India, I–II (Penguin Books, 1966). Vol. I, by R. Thapar, deals with the history of India before the arrival of the Mughals in 1526 A.D. Vol. II, by P. Spear, covers the period from 1526 to the present day.

K. A. Nilakanta Sastri, *History of India*, I–III, I. 3rd edition, II–III. 2nd edition (Madras, Viswanathan, Chetput, 1959–1964). A factual political history of Ancient, Muslim and British India.

J. C. Powell-Price, *A History of India, from the Earliest Times to 1939* (Reprint: London, Thomas Nelson & Sons, 1958).

V. A. Smith, *The Oxford History of India* (3rd corrected reprint of the 3rd edition by P. Spear: Oxford, Clarendon Press, 1967). This volume of almost 900 pages covers the entire history of India to 1947. Pt. I, Ancient and Hindu India, and pt. II, India in the Muslim period, are enlarged revisions by several authorities of the original edition; pt. III, India in the British period, is completely rewritten by P. Spear.

R. C. Majumdar, H. C. Raychaudhuri, and K. Datta, *An Advanced History of India* (Corrected reprint of the 2nd edition: New York, Macmillan & Co., 1958). This work of more than 1100 pages treats the entire history of India. Excellent maps and dynastic lists as well as bibliographies are appended to each chapter.

W. H. Moreland and A. C. Chatterjee, *A Short History of India*, 3rd edition (London, Longmans, Green & Co., 1953). A well-written survey of Indian history.

K. A. Nilakanta Sastri, *A History of South India, from Pre-historic Times to the Fall of Vijayanagar*, 3rd edition (Bombay, Oxford University Press, 1965). Written by one of the foremost scholars in the field.

R. C. Majumdar, *Ancient India*, revised edition (Delhi, Motilal Banarsidass, 1960). A survey of Indian history to 1200 A.D. by a specialist.

H. Raychaudhuri, *Political History of Ancient India, from the Accession of Parikshit to the Extinction of the Gupta Dynasty*, 6th revised edition (University of Calcutta, 1953). A detailed and carefully annotated handbook.

P. Spear, *India, A Modern History* (University of Michigan Press, 1961). A political history of Modern India including an extensive introductory account of the Ancient, Medieval and Muslim periods, with a useful section on suggested readings.

A. S. Altekar, *State and Government in Ancient India*, 3rd revised and enlarged edition (Delhi, Motilal Banarsidass, 1958). A comprehensive study of Indian polity before the Muslim conquest.

H. G. Rawlinson, *India, A Short Cultural History*, 5th impression (London, The Cresset Press; New York, Frederick A. Praeger, 1954). A lucid description of the various aspects of ancient and modern Indian culture.

A. L. Basham, *The Wonder That Was India, A Study of the Culture of the Indian Sub-Continent before the Coming of the Muslims*, 3rd revised edition (New York, Taplinger, 1968). A detailed reference work on early Indian culture with twelve most useful factual appendices.

Archaeology in India (Delhi, Dept. of Archaeology, Bureau of Education, publication no. 66, 1950). An excellent survey consisting of contributions by a number of specialists in different fields and techniques of Indian archaeology.

A. K. Coomaraswamy, *History of Indian and Indonesian Art*, unaltered republication of the 1st edition of 1927 (New York, Dover, 1965). A basic handbook on the history of Indian and South-East Asian art with 400 illustrations. In spite of the fact that this book was first published in 1927 it is still the most informative work on the subject due to its careful annotation and most valuable bibliography.

L. Frédéric, *L'Inde, ses temples — ses sculptures* (Paris, Arts et Métiers Graphiques, 1959). English edition *Indian Temples and Sculptures*, translated by E. M. Hooykaas and A. H. Christie (London, Thames and Hudson, 1959). A fine collection of 424 beautiful photographs illustrating the history of Indian art and architecture of the Prehistoric, Hindu-Buddhist, and Indo-Muslim periods. The pictures are arranged in chapters containing short introductions with maps as well as clear architectural plans and notes on each illustration.

D. Barrett and B. Gray, *Painting of India* (Cleveland, Albert Skira, 1963). A survey of the highlights of Indian painting incorporating the research of the past twenty years and illustrated with some 80 magnificent colour plates.

CEYLON

H. W. Codrington, *A Short History of Ceylon* (Reprint of the 2nd revised edition: London, Macmillan, 1947). Covers the history of Ceylon to 1833.

G. C. Mendis, *The Early History of Ceylon*, 9th imprint (Calcutta, Y.M.C.A., 1948). A short but excellent survey of ancient Ceylonese history, both political and cultural.

H. C. Ray and S. Paranavitana a.o., *History of Ceylon*, parts 1–2 (Ceylon University Press, 1959–1960). Basic handbook on the ancient history of Ceylon to 1505 A.D., including much information on its social and cultural aspects.

S. A. Pakeman, *Ceylon* (London, Ernest Benn, 1964). Treats the modern period of Ceylonese history.

W. Geiger, *Culture of Ceylon in Mediaeval Times*. Edited by H. Bechert (Wiesbaden, Otto Harrassowitz, 1960).

AFGHANISTAN

D. N. Wilber, *Annotated Bibliography of Afghanistan*, 3rd revised edition (New Haven, Human Relations Area Files Press, 1968). Contains a chapter on history with some 300 titles.

O. Caroe, *The Pathans, 550 B.C.–A.D. 1957* (Reprint of the 1st edition: London, Macmillan, 1962). A history of Afghanistan and North-West India focusing on the Pathan tribes.

W. K. Fraser-Tytler, *Afghanistan, A Study of Political Developments in Central and Southern Asia*, 2nd edition (Oxford University Press, 1953). A political history of Afghanistan mainly concerned with the period after 1747.

B. Rowland Jr., *Ancient Art from Afghanistan, Treasure of the Kabul Museum* (New York, The Asia Society, 1966). A beautiful exhibition catalogue concentrating on the Buddhist period of Afghanistan with a few plates illustrating prehistoric and Muslim objects.

TIBET

G. Schulemann, *Geschichte der Dalai-Lamas*, revised and enlarged edition (Leipzig, Otto Harrassowitz, 1958). An extensive and well-documented history of Tibet to the present day devoting considerable attention to religion and culture.

H. E. Richardson, *Tibet and its History* (Oxford University Press, 1962). A political history of Tibet mainly concerned with the period after 1720 A.D.

R. A. Stein, *La civilisation tibétaine* (Paris, Dunod, 1962). A scholarly survey of the history and culture of Tibet.

G. Tucci, *Tibet Land of Snows* (London, Elek Books, 1967). A beautifully illustrated account of Tibetan history and culture with 106 plates of which some 40 are in colour.

A. B. Griswold, Chewon Kim, and P. H. Pott, *Burma-Korea-Tibet* (London, Methuen, Art of the World Series, 1964). The third part of this book deals with Buddhism and Buddhist art objects in Tibet and contains 29 colour plates.

Luciano Petech, "Tibet", pp. 311–347 in *Geschichte Mittelasiens* (*Handbuch der Orientalistik*, edited by B. Spuler, Erste Abteilung, Fünfter Band, Fünfter Abschnitt, Leiden-Köln, E. J. Brill, 1966). A factual summary of Tibetan history.

NEPAL

D. R. Regmi, *Political and Economic History of Nepal from the Ancient Times to 1846 A.D.*, I–IV. I, Ancient Nepal; II, Medieval Nepal, pts. 1–3; III, Modern Nepal, Rise and Growth in the Eighteenth Century; IV, Bhim Sen to Mathabar (1800–1846) (Calcutta, K. L. Mukhopadhyay, 1959–1966). A handbook on the history of Nepal including its social and cultural aspects.

S. Kramrisch, *The Art of Nepal* (New York, The Asia Society, 1964). A beautifully illustrated survey of Nepalese sculpture and painting with nearly 100 illustrations.

SIKKIM

B. C. Olschak, *Sikkim, Himalajastaat zwischen Gletschern und Dschungeln* (Zürich, Schweizer Verlagshaus, 1965). A general introduction to Sikkim and its history with fine illustrations.

SOUTHEAST ASIA

D. G. E. Hall (editor), *Historians of South-East Asia* (Oxford University Press, 1961). Twenty-five contributions by various authors.

D. G. E. Hall, *A History of South-East Asia*, revised edition (London, Macmillan, 1964). Covers the complete history of

Southeast Asia with special reference to the period after the coming of the Europeans.

G. Coedès, *Les états hindouisés d'Indochine et d'Indonésie*, 3rd revised and enlarged edition (Paris, De Boccard, 1964). English edition *The Indianized States of Southeast Asia*, translated by S. B. Cowing (Honolulu, 1968). Treats the ancient history of Southeast Asia to 1511 A.D.

G. Coedès, *Les peuples de la péninsule indochinoise, histoire — civilisations* (Paris, Dunod, 1962). English edition *The Making of South-East Asia*, translated by H. M. Wright (London, 1966). Deals with the complete history of Southeast Asia with the exclusion of Malaya and Indonesia; special attention is paid to the period before the arrival of the Europeans.

B.-Ph. Groslier, *Hinterindien, Kunst im Schmelztiegel der Rassen* (Baden-Baden, Holle, Kunst der Welt, 1960). English edition *Indochina, Art in the Melting Pot of Races* (London, Methuen, Art of the World Series, 1962). A detailed survey of the history and art of Southeast Asia excluding Malaya and Indonesia, with 62 colour plates and 39 line-blocks.

R. Le May, *The Culture of South-East Asia*, 2nd edition (London, George Allen & Unwin, 1956). 3rd edition (Delhi, National Book Trust, 1962). A readable history of Southeast Asian art with good illustrations.

L. Frédéric, *Sud-Est Asiatique, ses temples — ses sculptures* (Paris, Arts et Métiers Graphiques, 1964). English edition *The Temples and Sculptures of South-East Asia* (London, Thames and Hudson, 1965). A beautiful picture book with full descriptions of the 454 plates arranged in chapters with short introductions to the history and art of each country.

BURMA

D. G. E. Hall, *Burma*, 3rd edition (London, Hutchinson University Library, 1960). A short survey of Burmese history from the beginning to 1960, devoted mainly to the period after the coming of the Europeans.

Maung Htin Aung, *A History of Burma* (Columbia University Press, 1967). A detailed history of Burma, dividing its attention equally between the ancient period and later times.

G. E. Harvey, *History of Burma from . the Earliest Times to*

10 March 1824, the Beginning of the English Conquest, 2nd imprint of the 1st edition of 1925 (London, Frank Cass, 1967).

V. C. Scott O'Connor, *Mandalay and Other Cities of the Past in Burma* (London, Hutchinson, 1907). An attractive description of the various ancient Burmese capitals, their architecture and cultural background, with many illustrations.

A. B. Griswold, Chewon Kim, and P. H. Pott, *Burma-Korea-Tibet* (London, Methuen, Art of the World Series, 1964). The first part of this book deals with Burmese art and architecture with a short historical introduction, and contains 10 colour plates and 30 line-blocks.

THAILAND

W. A. R. Wood, *History of Siam*, 3rd edition (Bangkok, Chalermnit, 1959). Deals with the history of Thailand from the earliest times to the present day.

R. B. Smith, *Siam, or the History of the Thais from the Earliest Times to 1824 A.D.*, I–II (Bethesda, Decatur Press, 1966–67).

Prince Damrong, *Siamese History Prior to the Founding of Ayudhya*, translated by J. Crosby (Bangkok, *Selected Articles from the Siam Society Journal*, Vol. III, pp. 36–100, 1959). Deals with the history of Thailand to 1350 A.D.

A. B. Griswold, *The Arts of Thailand, Handbook of the Architecture, Sculpture and Painting of Thailand (Siam), and a Catalogue of the Exhibition in the United States in 1960–61–62* (Indiana University, 1960). With 163 illustrations.

LAOS

M. L. Manich, *History of Laos (including the History of Lannathai, Chieng-mai)* (Bangkok, Chalermnit, 1967). Deals with the history of Laos and Northern Thailand from the beginning to the present day.

Maha Sila Viravong, *History of Laos* (Reprint: New York, Paragon, 1964). Discusses the history of Laos from the beginning to the middle of the nineteenth century.

H. Parmentier, *L'Art du Laos*, I–II (Paris and Hanoi, Publications de l'Ecole Française d'Extrême-Orient, XXXV, 1954). A detailed and extensive treatment of the art and architecture of Laos; vol. I, text; vol. II, 120 plates and 51 drawings.

CAMBODIA

M. Giteau, *Histoire du Cambodge* (Paris, Didier, 1957). A short but excellent summary of the history of Cambodia to the present day.

A. Migot, *Les Khmers, Des origines d'Angkor au Cambodge d'aujourd'hui* (Paris, Le Livre Contemporain, 1960). An extensive survey of Cambodian history.

S. Thierry, *Les Khmers* (Paris, Éditions du Seuil, 1964). A charmingly illustrated paperback on ancient Khmer history and culture.

L. Palmer Briggs, *The Ancient Khmer Empire* (Philadelphia, *Transactions of the American Philosophical Society*, NS, vol. 41, pt. I, 1951. Reprint 1955). An exhaustive manual of the ancient history and culture of the Khmers with excellent indices, a vast bibliography, and many figures, maps and plans.

J. Boisselier, *Le Cambodge, Manuel d'Archéologie d'Extrême-Orient*, Ière partie, tome I (Paris, Editions A. et J. Picard, 1966). An excellent treatment of the art and archaeology of Cambodia with extensive bibliography and indices, illustrated with 64 plates and 72 line-blocks.

B.-Ph. Groslier and J. Arthaud, *Angkor, hommes et pierres* (Paris, Arthaud, 1956). English revised and enlarged edition *Angkor, Art and Civilisation* (New York, Praeger, 1966). A beautiful picture book with more than 100 illustrations of the monuments in and around the ancient capital of Cambodia with short introductions on the historical and cultural background.

K. Krása and J. Cifra, *The Temples of Angkor, Monuments to a Vanished Empire* (London, Allan Wingate, 1963). Another excellent pictorial survey of the art and architecture of ancient Cambodia with a historical introduction to the 169 photographs.

M. Giteau, *Les Khmers, Sculptures khmères, Reflets de la civilisation d'Angkor* (Paris, Bibliothèque des Arts, 1965). English edition *Khmer Sculpture and Angkor Civilization* (Aspects of Art Series, I, 1965). A handbook on Khmer sculpture in stone, bronze, and wood with 26 magnificent colour plates and 235 illustrations in black and white.

CAMPĀ

G. Maspero, *Le royaume de Champa* (Paris and Brussels, G. Van Oest, 1928). A slightly antiquated history of Campā from the beginning to the conquest by Annam in 1471 A.D. For an up-to-date survey see numbers 2, 3, and 4 under Southeast Asia.

R. C. Majumdar, *Ancient Indian Colonies in the Far East*, vol. I, Champā (Lahore, Punjab Sanskrit Book Depot, 1927). For pt. 1, same comment as for the previous item; pt. 2 deals with religion, society, art, and architecture; pt. 3 gives the text and translation of 130 inscriptions.

Ph. Stern, *L'art du Champa (Ancien Annam) et son évolution* (Toulouse, Les Frères Douladoure, 1942).

MALAYA

R. O. Winstedt, *A History of Malaya*, revised and enlarged edition (Singapore, Marican & Sons, 1962). On the history of Malaya from the beginning to the present day dealing mainly with the period after the coming of the Europeans.

P. Wheatley, *Impressions of the Malay Peninsula in Ancient Times* (Singapore, Eastern University Press, 1964). Deals with Malayan history to the conquest of Malacca in 1511 A.D.

H. Miller, *The Story of Malaysia* (London, Faber and Faber, 1965). A history of the Federation of Malaya concerned mainly with the period after 1511 A.D.

R. O. Winstedt, *The Malays, A Cultural History*, 6th edition (London, Routledge & Kegan Paul, 1961). Discusses various aspects of Malay culture.

INDONESIA

Soedjatmoko a.o., *An Introduction to Indonesian Historiography* (Cornell University Press, 1965). Twenty-two contributions by various authors.

B. H. M. Vlekke, *Nusantara, A History of Indonesia*, 4th revised edition (The Hague, W. van Hoeve, 1959). An extensive survey of the colonial history of Indonesia to the Japanese conquest, with a short introduction to the period preceding the arrival of the Europeans.

N. J. Krom, *Hindoe-Javaansche Geschiendenis*, 2nd revised

edition (The Hague, Martinus Nijhoff, 1931). The basic handbook of ancient Indonesian history, in Dutch.

R. C. Majumdar, *Ancient Indian Colonies in the Far East*, vol. II, Suvarnadvipa, pts. 1–2 (Dacca, A. K. Majumdar, 1937–38). A detailed account of ancient Indonesian history. Pt. 1 deals with political history; pt. 2 treats the various aspects of ancient Indonesian culture.

B. R. Chatterji, *History of Indonesia, Early and Mediaeval*, 3rd edition (Meerut, Meenakshi Prakashan, 1967). A short summary of ancient Indonesian history devoting special attention to literature; pp. 107–198 give the text and translation of a number of inscriptions.

C. Holt, *Art in Indonesia, Continuities and Change* (Cornell University Press, 1967). An excellent survey of ancient and modern Indonesian art including dance and drama, with 200 illustrations.

A. J. Bernet Kempers, *Ancient Indonesian Art* (Harvard University Press, 1959). A fine pictorial survey of Indo-Javanese art and architecture with a short introduction and detailed notes on the 353 plates.

J. E. van Lohuizen - de Leeuw

CHINA

How can the past of China (and of course of other parts of the Orient as well) be integrated with occidental history? That such a problem exists is apparent if one looks at so-called world histories that have been written. The more academic sort scarcely mentions China or the Far East at all until the expansion of Europe in modern times; a few writers have been more venturesome but they have generally come to grief through the sheer unmanageableness of so much rich and varied material or have failed through attempting to reduce it to order by forcing it into an inadequate and unsuited conceptual framework based on *a priori* considerations or derived from accepted notions of western history. One has considerable sympathy for the scholar, whether orientalist or historian, who prefers to cultivate his own field without bothering about what is over the fence. Nevertheless I think it is highly desirable that scholars in each discipline should occasionally look over the fence or even try to break it down, so as to restore in the world of the imagination the continuity of the real world, which never ceases to exist however much we compartmentalise our knowledge. For the Far East *is* part of our world and has always been part of our world. Not only is this true in the physical sense that contact and inter-action have existed from time immemorial; but man in China is basically the same as man everywhere else and the experience of the Chinese, or of other oriental peoples, can be as valid and useful for us as that of the Greeks and Romans or, for that matter, of the Europeans who are our immediate ancestors. If it can be said that one of the purposes of history is to help us to understand the nature of man with all its limitations and potentialities then we have not fully appreciated our task if we leave Chinese man out of account.

I was originally asked to write on the whole Far East. If I confine myself to China I do so merely because whatever competence I have lies wholly in that field and not because

I wish to imply that the other Far Eastern nations, Korea, Annam and Japan, which have adopted the Chinese script and based so much of their civilisation on China, have any less interest for the general historian. For another limitation I have no apology. I shall deal only with the Han Chinese of China proper, by which I mean not a "race" or "nation" (in the European sense), but the people who through history have been the creators and bearers of the distinctive Chinese civilisation, leaving out of consideration the peoples of Tibet, Sinkiang, Mongolia and Manchuria before its fairly recent settlement by the Chinese, even though these territories have been politically joined to China for some centuries. For although the nations which have adopted the Chinese script have many basic features in common so that however divergent they may be in some respects they can be called one family, the other border peoples, whose use of alphabetic scripts of Indian or Near Eastern origin is a mark of their fundamentally different cultural patterns, have remained merely neighbours and belong properly to another story. One cannot ignore the neighbours! The peoples of Inner Asia have on the whole had much closer relations with China and much greater influence on her history than have her daughter cultures. Nevertheless they form part of my topic only in this way, as external forces, and not for their importance in themselves.

So far as our present evidence can tell us, Chinese civilisation appears in North China in the latter half of the second millenium B.C. The discovery at An-yang in Honan province, almost within the present century, of thousands of bone and tortoise-shell fragments, many of them inscribed, the refuse of a form of divination practised by the ancient Chinese kings, has provided us with the earliest examples of Chinese writing and confirmed in a striking and quite unexpected way the existence of the Shang dynasty (traditional dates: 1766—1123 B.C. or preferably 1523—1027) which sceptics were beginning to look upon as wholly legendary. To the present no such confirmation has been found for the reality of the Hsia dynasty which tradition places before the Shang, still less for the sage kings who preceded the Hsia, and we are left in our search for origins to make what we can of the unlettered neolithic cultures whose remains have been discovered here and there in North China. Was an impulse, however indirect, from the ancient civilisations of the Near East responsible for the first beginnings of the bronze-using, literate culture which we find in full flower in the Shang remains? We have as yet little evidence beyond what we may think of the inherent probabilities to enable us to answer this question and it is perhaps best to restrain speculation.

This early Chinese civilisation, as we find it at the beginning of the first millenium B.C. when the Shang state was conquered by the "barbarian" Chou people from Shensi, seems to have been confined to the lower Yellow River plain with extensions southwards towards the Huai and the Yangtze and westward and northward along the Wei and Fen valleys in Shensi and Shansi respectively. All around and in between more or less isolated Chinese islands were the barbarians, probably of similar racial stocks to the Chinese but at a more primitive cultural level. Throughout the Chou dynasty (1027–256 B.C.), the great formative age of Chinese civilisation, the various feudal states into which China was then divided expanded by conquest and absorption of the barbarians. By the time of the unification by Ch'in in 221 B.C. the cultural frontiers had been extended in the north to the edge of the steppe, eastward to the sea in Shantung and southward to the Huai, along the Han and into Szechwan. At the same time originally non-Chinese peoples along the Yangtze had been drawn into the Chinese cultural orbit and developed into Chinese states. In Han (206 B.C.–219 A.D.) the centre of Chinese culture was still in the north and the Yangtze valley was on the periphery. In T'ang (618–906) Fukien and Kwangtung were still remote outposts, and it was only in the Sung dynasty (960–1279) that the Yangtze valley came to outweigh the north in population and economic importance. Even to-day the process of sinicisation is far from complete in Kwangsi, Yunnan, Kweichow and the remoter parts of Szechwan, and groups of aboriginal peoples such as the Miaotzu, Lolos and Mosos resist absorption into the politically dominant culture around them.

The history of the northern frontier since the Chou period has been very different. To the south the colonising Chinese always found lands suited to his form of settled agriculture and inhabited by people practising agriculture of the same basic pattern, even if less advanced technically and socially. When he came to the steppe lands of the north and west however, he found an environment which admitted of no such exploitation. Here the nomadic herdsman reigned supreme. The conflict between these two ways of life was never resolved. The Great Wall, first completed (not along its present course) by the First Emperor of Ch'in by linking together the frontier walls erected against the nomads by the separate states, stands as a symbol of the separation of the two worlds. Equally symbolic is the stubborn resistance of the nomads to Chinese culture and their preference for Near Eastern or Indian cultural influences.

While the area of Chinese civilisation has gradually widened in its homeland, it has been adopted, as has already been mentioned, by three neighbouring lands which have retained their own spoken languages and many underlying characteristics but have based their higher cultures on China. Korea and Annam both came under Chinese domination in the Ch'in-Han period and might have suffered the same fate of gradual colonisation and absorption that befell the southern provinces of China if communications had been easier to maintain and China had continuously had a strong centralised power able to exert its control. As it was, Korea became independent in the 4th century A.D. and Annam in the 10th. In both cases, however, independence did not mean the rejection of the culture of the erstwhile conqueror but rather its assimilation by the native peoples themselves. Japan on the other hand was never under Chinese rule. As she emerged from barbarism and became a united nation in the 3rd and 4th centuries A.D. the first elements of higher culture came to her from sinicised Korea. Then after the Sui, followed by the T'ang, had put an end to the period of disunity known as the Northern and Southern Dynasties and China became once more a resplendent power dominating the whole of East Asia, Japan set herself to emulating Chinese culture with a speed and energy comparable only to her westernisation in the 19th century. The process was not complete, of course, and in the centuries that followed there was reaction in favour of native things and much indigenous development. Yet if one looks at Japanese culture to-day one is perhaps more in danger of not seeing fully what is native than of failing to note the immense Chinese contribution.

I have already mentioned two essential characteristics of Chinese civilisation, its script and its economic reliance on agriculture. The gentleman scholar to instruct and command and the peasant to till the soil, these were the two divisions of society with an unquestioned usefulness that stood at the top of the theoretical social scale. Other types of economic activity, those of the craftsman and merchant, were looked upon, sometimes with downright hostility, sometimes with a rational recognition of their necessity in a complex society, but always as the "branches" which must be carefully watched and pruned if necessary, lest they should grow at the expense of the root activity of agriculture. It is true that we owe some of the greatest triumphs of Chinese civilisation to its craftsmen, and even commerce, the most suspect activity of all, made advances of world historical significance, but ultimately the attitude of the Confucian bureaucracy could not help having a serious inhibiting effect.

In theory and in practice agriculture has always been the livelihood of the vast majority of the Chinese. It has moreover largely been agriculture of a narrowly limited type concentrating on the intensive growing of food grains on small holdings. No doubt the present degree of intensity has only been reached after centuries of gradual development but it would seem that in the earliest times of which we have record peasant families individually tilled small fields to produce food grains. Migratory slash and burn cultivation was already dying out in early historical times and was being replaced by settled cultivation with the the use of fallowing. A technical revolution was brought about by the introduction of iron implements from about the end of the 4th century B.C. and it has been argued that this enabled a favoured few to exploit land on a more extensive scale, with the use also of oxen for ploughing and improved techniques of irrigation.

However this may be, and the evidence is very scanty, a permanent change did gradually come about at this time in the form of land ownership and the way in which the surplus product was drawn off. The no doubt idealised *ching-t'ien* or "well-field" system, looked upon as the primeval form of land tenure, seems to reflect the reality of a village community of peasants sharing the available land out among themselves and cultivating a portion of it in common for the benefit of the local lord. Before the unification by Ch'in (221 B.C.) however, the private ownership of extensive tracts had begun to appear. Yet it would seem that it remained typical to exploit one's estate by letting plots to tenants, who no doubt tilled the land much as did the independent peasants, rather than by working it as a unit with gangs of slaves or hired labourers.

This is disputed by some but even if they are right and there was a certain amount of large-scale farming, it had no lasting effect. Later technical improvements—improved varieties, better manuring, the introduction of other crops such as tea and cotton—never altered the basic pattern of individual peasant agriculture and only served to make it more intensive and to reduce the size of the holdings.

The ways in which the surplus was drawn off for the benefit of the ruling classes also showed considerable elaboration in the course of the centuries. The landlord and the mandarin demanding taxes for the central government took the place of the local lord but the relationship of the peasant to his new masters was conceived in much the same terms as had been his relationship to his old master. Yet if there was no sharp break there was a gradual evolution in this as in other aspects of Chinese life and the position of the peasant undoubtedly did improve, both in theory and in practice, over the centuries. This is noticeable, for instance, in the gradual replacement of demands for direct labour services, whether from the government or from the landlord, by fixed rents in kind and, increasingly, in money.

The upper class (I use this term loosely for lack of a better one) underwent more profound changes in its composition and way of life than did the peasantry. In early historical times we find society sharply divided into a hereditary ruling

caste and the subject masses.   The 'patricians' consisted of a
limited number of great exogamous clans.   Their religion,
involving the cult of heaven and of the family and clan
ancestors, was not shared by the common people.   War and
hunting played a large part in their lives but they, or rather,
no doubt, specialised groups among them, were also the
custodians of the written language and of the traditional lore
embodied in it—historical traditions, songs, rites and the arts
of divination, etc.   One may imagine that these clerkly
pursuits were left to the more humble members of the aristocratic clans but, if so, they had their revenge.   For it was
the ethics and political theory elaborated by these learned
scribes that Confucius was concerned to preserve and transmit
to posterity and that were to grow through the centuries into
the system we know as Confucianism which formed the
foundation of Chinese society until yesterday.   These early
pre-Confucians developed the rational, ethical ideal of the
ruler, the Son of Heaven, holding the mandate of heaven but
not himself divine, and capable of being supplanted if his
conduct became such as to forfeit this high mandate.   Theirs
too was the ideal of the supremacy of learning and of the
perfect scholar and gentleman, of however humble (patrician)
origin, scrupulously and rationally basing his conduct on the
examples handed down from the sages of old and ready to
follow out his principles even at the risk of his life, which
became the accepted standard (however much they fell from
it in practice) of the scholar mandarins of imperial China.

In the troubled course of the economic and cultural expansion
of the Chou period the original sharp division of society by
birth disappeared.   The old aristocracy died out or decayed
and sank into the plebeian masses.   Wealth and power came
into the hands of new men who often repudiated violently the
old politics and ethics.   Yet in the end a part of the old
patrician norms was extended to the whole population and
preserved its continuity even in the new, radically different
society.   To-day *pai-hsing* 'the hundred clans' does not mean
the aristocracy but rather the peasantry, and the system of
exogamy is universal.   In this we see an example of the
conservative adaptation which has been typical of Chinese

history, dramatically symbolised at the beginning of the imperial era by the failure of the root and branch revolution of Ch'in and the success of Han, which accomplished the same end of imperial unification more slowly by accepting and re-interpreting tradition.

It took many centuries of evolution however before the ideal of government through a bureaucracy selected solely on the basis of learning, without regard to wealth or birth, reached even the degree of fulfilment that so astonished Europeans in China from the 16th century onward. The Han period, which saw the final disappearance of the remnants of the old feudal order, also saw the growth of powerful new landed families which came, in the centuries of disorder and division which followed the Han, to have exclusive aristocratic pretensions. The examination system, though arising out of earlier institutions, only really comes into being in the Sui-T'ang period (580–906 A.D.) and even then the principle of rule by an aristocracy of birth remained for centuries its strong rival. But the interest of the central government was always against having hereditary power of any kind outside the imperial house and this, combining with the Confucian scholar ethic, gradually brought about the state of affairs in Ming and Ch'ing which European enthusiasts such as Leibnitz and Voltaire looked upon as the rule of the philosophers come true, but which, alas, has also given rise to all the evil connotations of the word "mandarin" in our language.

Another continuing feature of Chinese history which distinguishes it especially from India, but also by its persistence and strength from most other parts of the world, was the ideal of the political unity of 'All under Heaven'. It is present in the earliest political theorising and appears as a universally accepted presupposition of all the many brands of philosophy that appeared in the Spring and Autumn and Warring States Periods (8th to 3rd centuries B.C.), the time in all Chinese history when it was least realised in practice. The achievement of unity by Ch'in, not as the feudally gradated decentralised unity which the Confucians had idealised, but in the form of the egalitarian despotism favoured by the Legalists, fatefully set the standard for the following two millenia, even though a new syncretic Confucianism and not Legalism emerged as the official doctrine of the new state. In spite of periods, sometimes protracted, when there was more than one claimant to the title of Son of Heaven, or when the commands of the acknowledged Son of Heaven were little heeded, the ideal of unity never ceased to be accepted and the type of state created by Ch'in and Han was continually renewed. The institutions of later dynasties developed with no sharp break in continuity out of those of their predecessors, and different as 19th century China was from the China of the 2nd century B.C., it had undergone no political revolution in the meanwhile of the magnitude of that carried out by the First Emperor of Ch'in.

Apart from the great edifice of ethics and political theory which is perhaps their greatest creation, much of China's artistic achievement is also stamped, or rather penetrated through and through, with the mark of the scholar bureaucracy. I am thinking principally of the arts based on the written character, whether in its meaningful content or in its aesthetic form—that is, of literature in all its branches, of calligraphy, and also of a great deal of Chinese painting. In the arts we frequently see the Taoist obverse of the medal—playfulness, scepticism, acceptance, non-activity, naturalism, mysticism—to set against the high seriousness, activism and down-to-earthness of the Confucian face.

The main stream of higher Chinese culture, whether Confucian or Taoist, is of native growth but has never lacked influence from outside. The period in which China was most receptive to foreign things was the 1000 years following the discovery of the west by Chang Ch'ien (after 139 B.C.). New ideas came freely into China from India and the Iranian world and many of them were absorbed into Chinese civilisation. Buddhism was much the most important of these influences and though the religion itself was always regarded with some suspicion by the most orthodox mandarins, it did sometimes manage to rival Confucianism for the allegiance of the upper classes and it penetrated deeply both into the later Taoist religion and the neo-Confucian philosophy of Sung. Needless to say through its influence on the literate classes

Buddhism has had profound effects on all Chinese art forms.

Indian and Iranian influences were not confined to the ruling classes. From the rising of the Yellow Turbans at the end of the Later Han dynasty (184 A.D.) to the Taipings and the Boxers of the 19th century, popular religious sects have constantly appeared in Chinese history as fomenters of revolt against the existing social order and frequently the religion has been one of foreign origin or has contained foreign elements. The earliest of all, the Revolt of the Yellow Turbans, is on the face of it a purely Chinese phenomenon since one of their leaders, Chang Lu, is the reputed ancestor of the later Taoist popes and their sect has clearly some close relation to the later Taoist religion. Yet it is recognised that the organisation of the Taoist church owed much to the example of Buddhism, already becoming known in China in the 1st and 2nd centuries A.D. In later, similar phenomena messianic ideas derived from Buddhism and Manichaeism are patently visible and in the 19th century Christianity added a new ingredient to the mixture. Such extraneous religious ideas provided a positive ideology which a revolting peasantry could match against the Confucianism of the mandarins; but they were never able to create a *political* idea which could adequately supplant the existing order and in the end the mandarins won out, even if it was to a greater or less degree a new set of mandarins.

The lower orders of society, however, contributed much more than lost causes to Chinese history and culture. Nameless for the most part are the craftsmen whose products have excited the admiration of the world. One need only begin to mention bronzes, jades, ceramics, lacquer, silks . . . to evoke in each case countless visual delights. The glory of the Chinese artisan is based on mundane and practical things as well, for it is to his ingenuity that we owe many of the inventions on which modern world civilisation is based. Paper, printing, gun-powder and the mariner's compass are the most famous but the list can perhaps be extended to include such things as the drawloom, the stern post rudder, the wheel barrow, the art of casting iron, the iron plough-share.

To be sure, Chinese inventiveness stopped short of industrial machinery such as has transformed European and world civilisation in the last two hundred years. Perhaps part of the reason for this was that the supply of cheap manpower made it unnecessary to look for power from the forces of nature. No doubt also the orthodox physiocratic philosophy had a very inhibiting effect. Thus, when water mills were introduced they were bitterly opposed by the Coufucian mandarins on the grounds that they interfered with the use of water for irrigation and encouraged "branch" activities. Emphasis on intuitive skill of hand and eye and a consequent attitude of indifference or hostility towards abstract analysis, so typical of the Taoist side of the Chinese, combined with the Confucian down-to-earth social emphasis, were perhaps reflected equally in Chinese artistic achievement and practical ingenuity, and in their failure to develop very far in mathematics or abstract science. But much remains to be found out about these questions.

The merchant too, in spite of his theoretically low status, has also achieved a great deal, besides playing an important, though usually obscure, role through Chinese history. The history of Chinese banking and commercial practice has yet to be written but one development, the early use of paper money, is well known. Other forms of banking paper had been devised as early as the beginning of the 9th century and it is not impossible that they were influential in stimulating developments elsewhere.

As with primitive industrialism, the activities of merchants were hemmed in by the regulations of a suspicious bureaucracy. Chinese walled cities, unlike their European counterparts, never became centres of mercantile freedom. They existed in the first place as the residence of the local lord—and the mandarin, his successor. Markets there were, but closely supervised and policed by the government. In the T'ang period trading inside the cities was still restricted to the hours of daylight and to defined market areas in which merchants of a given type were kept together and held mutually responsible for each other's conduct. From Sung times onward city life became much freer but merchants still found it convenient to band themselves together to preserve their monopoly. Conversely the government found such groups useful for purposes of control and levying imposts. This is the probable origin of the Chinese merchant gilds which remained a feature of Chinese life up to the present. Whatever their economic power and their importance along with the clan and similar institutions as self-regulating organisations at the base of Chinese society, they never attempted to demand 'liberties' or to assert 'rights', still less to take part in government.

*   *   *

In mentioning the artistic and technological creations of Chinese civilisation, we leave the experience of man in China and come to China's influence, through history, on the rest of the world. The first indisputable knowledge of China appears in the west in the last century B.C. when Serica, the land of silk, begins to find its way into Greek and Latin writings, and it was pre-eminently as the home of this product that China was for long known. The reason for the establishment of contact at this time must have been the expansion into Central Asia of the Han dynasty seeking strategic bases and allies against its nomad enemies, the Hsiung-nu, and the consequent opening up of the caravan route through the oases of Turkestan. This great Silk Road was for centuries the main link between the Far East and the Roman world. Along it came not only silk but also other products such as Siberian furs, ginger and Chinese cast iron. Scraps of knowledge about the great empires at either end of the road also penetrated in each direction and made their way into the classical geographers such as Strabo and Ptolemy on the one hand and into the Chinese official accounts of foreign countries on the other. The reference to 'atheistic Chinese' ($\Sigma\hat{\eta}\rho\epsilon\varsigma$ $o\acute{\iota}$ $\overset{\prime}{\alpha}\theta\epsilon o\iota$) in Origen's *Contra Celsum* even suggests that some vague rumours about Confucianism had made their way with the merchant caravans.

The politics of the Silk Road and Chinese relations with their nomad neighbours in general must also have played a part in causing the great movements of peoples across Eurasia which made themselves felt in the Near East and in Europe in successive waves for centuries.   It may be doubted whether such an exact correlation as one scholar has suggested can be established between the frontier wars of the Chinese and those of the Romans—as if the steppe were a fluid obeying the principle that pressure on any point is transferred equally in all directions to the other points on the surface; and our ignorance may prevent us from ever reaching certainty, especially about the early centuries.   Nevertheless it may be permissible to infer from what we know of the Turks and the Mongols that in the case of earlier peoples also events along the Great Wall of China sometimes had repercussions sooner or later, perhaps in North India or Iran, perhaps in Russia.

By the 2nd and 3rd centuries A.D. a southern sea route had opened up from India and the west around Malaya to the ports of Annam and south China.   By this route we hear for the first time of the arrival in China of subjects of Rome, self-styled ambassadors of An-tun (Marcus Aurelius Antoninus). In the opposite direction new and more exact knowledge of Far Eastern geography came to Rome.   The name China in the forms Thīnaī, Sīnai and later Tzinitza came through India and represents Sanskrit Cīna, Cīnasthāna, which in turn is most probably derived from Ch'in, the name of the state in what is now Shensi province in north-west China which united China in its first imperial dynasty from 221 to 206 B.C.

The instability and troubles of China from the 3rd to the end of the 6th century A.D. did not put an end to contacts with the outside world.   The spread of Buddhism in those centuries indeed greatly stimulated interest in India and the Buddhist centres of Central Asia and there was much travel in either direction by both the sea and the land routes.   With the rise of Islam in the Near East a flourishing sea-borne commerce grew up between the Caliphate and South China ports. Arab, Persian and Jewish merchants came in such numbers that they formed a considerable colony living permanently at Canton in the 9th century; and Chinese junks were a familiar sight in the Persian gulf.   A Moslem writer of the 9th century lists among products of China : silk goods, silk, pottery, paper, ink, peacocks, good running horses, saddles, felt, cinnamon, unmixed Greek rhubarb, gold and silver utensils, drugs, brocades, female slaves, figurines, inviolable locks, hydraulic engineers, agricultural experts, masons and eunuchs.

In the 8th century the T'ang empire and the expanding Caliphate came for a time into direct contact in Central Asia. In 751 the Arabs and their allies won a victory over the Chinese and theirs at the Battle of Talas and though China's internal troubles and not this defeat were mainly responsible for the decline of her influence in Turkestan thereafter, the battle itself did have an important consequence in that Chinese prisoners taken on that occasion introduced the art of paper-making to the Near East. The secret of silk production had become known some centuries earlier.

With the decline of the T'ang dynasty at the end of the 9th century, there was a temporary disruption of trade relations with the Near East but with the rise of Sung after 960 the sea route at any rate began to flourish again more than ever. The overland route was less flourishing because of the anarchic state of the steppe lands in which there was no strong power to maintain secure communications.

The sudden irruption of the Mongols in the 13th century which established for a short period a single empire stretching from Iraq and South Russia to the Pacific Ocean established ease and security between the west and the Far East such as had never before existed and were never to exist again until modern times. For the first time Europeans visited China, marvelled at its wealth and civilisation and wrote down accounts for their fellows at home to read. Thus was born the legend of Cathay which was to haunt European minds for centuries after the Mongol empire had dissolved and with it the possibility of making contact with the fabulous world beyond the Tartar wastes.

The Mongol epoch must also have opened the way for knowledge of the art of printing, surely the greatest of Chinese inventions, to come to Europe. Block printing originated among the Buddhists, apparently as a means of multiplying holy images and sutras, and was known already in the T'ang period. Secular printing began in the 10th century and became increasingly common in the Sung dynasty. Although the nature of Chinese writing with its multiplicity of signs favoured the method of printing from wooden blocks, methods of printing from movable type are known to have been devised in the Sung period and there was large-scale printing from movable metal type in Korea at the beginning of the 15th century. Although the way in which knowledge of printing was transmitted to Europe is obscure—perhaps vague reports were sufficient to stimulate curious and inventive minds—it would surely be asking too much of coincidence to make it account for an entirely independent development of printing in 15th century Europe, so soon after the Mongols had provided the possibility of contact with China. The use of gunpowder in war was also taken to Europe from China by the Mongols, even if doubts may remain about who was responsible for the invention of the cannon.

At last, in the 16th century, partly inspired by the Cathay legend, came the Portuguese around Africa and the Spaniards across the Pacific. In an increasing stream the products of the Far East made their way into European ports and with them came more and more information, often superficial no doubt but often surprisingly exact, about China and its neighbours. With the traders came the missionaries and above all the scholar Jesuits, who managed to make an entrance into the xenophobic Ming empire and establish themselves in Peking itself. There they were eventually accepted by the Chinese court for their mathematical and scientific, particularly astronomical, learning, but perhaps even more because of their willingness to adapt themselves to the ways of the Chinese scholar class and to immerse themselves in Chinese learning. Through their enthusastic reports, no doubt distorted by their ecclesiastical preoccupations, there came to the west for the first time some knowledge of Chinese history and philosophy, to the intense excitement of such European thinkers as Leibnitz and Voltaire. While the sinomania of the 18th century both in art and in philosophy was based on very false notions of what was Chinese, the Chinese inspiration behind it cannot be ignored. Confucianism had never been the pure, primeval monotheism that the Jesuits thought they saw in it and that Voltaire identified with deism, the rule of the scholar mandarins had never deserved quite the enthusiastic praise it sometimes got, nor had China ever realised the physiocratic ideal which so much appealed to Quesnay. Yet all these ideas had some foundation in fact; and merely to know of the existence on the other side of the world of a large, populous, well-governed and civilised empire based on totally different principles from those of Erope must have been very stimulating to 17th and 18th century minds. In a more prosaic and practical but no less important way it has been suggested that Chinese ideas of state organisation influenced developments in the Prussian bureaucracy as they later influenced the reform of the British Civil Service.

The new Europe of the 19th century, full of confidence in its own progress and easily out of patience with the stiff, proud conservatism and weak corruption of the declining Manchu dynasty, was less ready to see virtue in Chinese civilisation. By their brusque forcing of Chinese exclusiveness, however, Europeans were for the first time able to get to know China and the Chinese at first hand. Superficial knowledge about China became more and more common and a few persons were able to obtain the means for more profound studies.

At the same time European penetration into East Asiatic waters brought China and her neighbours willy-nilly into the European system of international relations, grown to a world system. At first they were the passive objects of European expansionism and rivalries but in an astonishingly short time Japan emerged as a world power and now, after a long travail, China has done the same. In the mid-twentieth century the Far East has become as important in world politics as Europe.

It would be an illusion to suppose that because Japan, China, and now Korea and Annam, have entered the contemporary world as states on European models they have abruptly discarded their past or that a knowledge of their historic cultures will not be essential for understanding them in future. It would be rash to predict what the elements of continuity will be or how they will enter into the renewed societies that are emerging in the Far East but it can be confidently asserted that there will be a great deal of continuity. This of course argues for more study of the historic cultures of the Far East on our part. At the same time when our confidence in the superiority of the west has been shaken it seems possible that we might ourselves draw on the experience of man in the Far East more than we have yet done.

*   *   *

Granted that the western historian ought to know more about Chinese history, what are his chances of finding out what he wants? The western historian may rightly demand that before sinologists accuse him of failing to take their field into account they must make available material in a language and form that he can use. Though one can point to many cases where available material about China has been ignored, one must on the whole admit that this demand has so far not been adequately met. A brief survey of the nature of the sources for Chinese history may help to show some of the difficulties which lie in the way of meeting it.

The first and most formidable obstacle is the immense quantity and variety of the existing sources, especially when compared to the small number of workers in the field. It has been said that before the 19th century there was more printed books in China than in the rest of the world put together. If one interprets history in the widest sense to include social and cultural history, all of this, including poems, essays, commentaries on the classics, encyclopedias, short stories, drama, novels, etc.—and all that has been added since—is relevant; but even if one confines oneself to strictly historical writing and documentation, the amount is enormous. One naturally thinks first of the 24 (or 25 or 26) standard histories, a daunting bulk of Chinese text, which give a continuous account of Chinese history from legendary times to the beginning of the republic and represent an unbroken tradition of official history writing of 2000 years. The first of them, the Shih-chi or "Historical Records" of Ssu-ma Ch'ien (completed ca. 80 B.C.) established the essentials of the pattern—(1) "basic annals" giving a brief chronicle of the main events by the reigns of emperors; (2) "biographies" of important personnages (including also accounts of foreign countries); (3) "monographs" containing material on administrative matters such as the calendar, rites, geography, economics, etc., arranged topically;

(4) "tables" of genealogies and other matters conveniently presented in such a form.*

Works of a historical nature, some of them still extant, existed centuries before Ssu-ma Ch'ien and provided the source material for his work. He started his history with the earliest traditions that he considered credible and came down to his own day. Pan Ku, however, who compiled his Han-shu on the same model, made it the account of a single, defunct dynasty and other standard histories are mostly the same in this. In a few cases the histories of a limited series of short-lived dynasties are included in a single work. In later times it became the rule that each dynasty compiled an official standard history of its predecessor from material preserved in that dynasty's archives and already arranged in the form of True Records of each reign.

For the last two dynasties, the Ming (1368–1644) and the Ch'ing (1644–1912), the True Records, running into many hundreds of volumes, are preserved and have been published, and an immense amount of other archive material is also in existence. Less has come down from earlier times but even for them the standard histories represent only a fraction of what is at our disposal. Numerous chronologically arranged histories have been prepared, sometimes under official auspices, sometimes privately, covering longer or shorter periods. Some merely rearrange and summarise what is in the standard histories but others preserve much additional information and must now be treated as primary sources. Private or official accounts of particular events exist in abundance, especially for later times.

Administrative and legal codes, collections and digests of official documents, gazetteers, etc., exist for all periods from the T'ang onwards. Especially interesting and important are the local gazetteers. The earliest extant specimen comes from the 4th century A.D. and fragments exist from the T'ang period, but most existing specimens date from Ming and Ch'ing. By the 19th century there were gazetteers for every province,

---

* The Shih-chi also contained a section known as Shih-chia on the hereditary ruling families of feudal states which does not normally appear in later dynastic histories. The names given to the different sections were not always the same and several histories do not have monographs or tables.

every prefecture and sub-prefecture and sometimes for smaller territorial divisions as well, containing historical as well as topographical and administrative information. Important too are the genealogies and family histories that have been preserved by the various clans.

Since most men who wrote anything at all were officials at some time or other and it was usual to include all a man's writings, official as well as private, in his collected works, a very large part of Chinese prose literature consists of historical documents of essentially the same kind as are contained in what are formally classified as historical books. Memorials to the throne on topics of the day, decrees and official letters composed while in office, official obituary notices or private epitaphs of other officials are all to be found alongside poems, philosophical essays, private letters, miscellaneous jottings, etc., in a man's works. Even the letters and poems, since they were so often addressed to fellow officials or occasioned by some official event, sometimes allow us to check or enlarge statements in the histories.

Whether produced officially by the central government or by a local government office or unofficially by a private literatus, all writings of the sort I have been discussing have certain common features. They all bear the stamp of the unique Chinese combination of learning and bureaucracy, in short of the Confucian mandarin. Hence their overwhelming preoccupation with politics and administration and their scant attention to aspects of life which did not often come to the notice of the bureaucrats such as religion, industry and trade. Hence the punctilious attention to correct formal distinctions in language, as for instance in referring to the emperor. Hence the moralising comments—though it is easy to exaggerate the influence of 'praise and blame' in practice.

Buddhism, in spite of its Indian origin, produced in China a historiography imitative of the Confucian model. Though often full of marvels and miracles it goes some way to make up for the meagre treatment given to that religion in secular works. Taoism on the contrary has produced no historiography.

A universal characteristic of Chinese historical writing is its impersonality. The typical historiographical method, deliberately and consciously followed by the author of the first standard history, Ssu-ma Ch'ien, was to piece together quotations from earlier works, sometimes in abbreviated or simplified form, but with a minimum of connective material and a clear separation of any brief interpretative or moralising comment on the part of the compiler. This did not mean that criticism was not exercised in the selection of material, but criticism was necessarily restricted to choosing between contradictory versions of the same event or eliminating what seemed obviously irrational or impossible. There was little attempt to divine the implications of the statements in one's sources and to use them as the means of making one's own imaginative reconstruction of past events.

The fact that Chinese histories are so largely compilations of course enhances their value as sources for modern historians who are not satisfied with them as histories. Paradoxically it often makes works which have been criticised by earlier generations of Chinese as being hastily flung together and lacking in literary excellence of more use than much praised books in which the compilers have carefully improved the style of their sources and edited or abridged them according to strict principles. Impersonality and verbatim transcription of source material compensate to a great extent for the loss of the actual original documents, though one must of course be on one's guard against corruption in transmission and misunderstanding that can arise through editorial abridgement or the piecing together of unrelated documents in a misleading way. One is moreover at the mercy of the editor for his selection of documents, at least in earlier periods when supplementing material is scarce.

Original documents are by no means lacking. In a wide sense every material object, inscribed or not, produced by a culture has evidential value. The Chinese have been connoisseurs and antiquarians for a very long time, carefully collecting works of art and other relics of the past, writing about them and establishing a rich tradition of learning and criticism on to which modern scholarship can build. Systematic archaeology is a comparatively recent innovation brought in from outside but it has already produced spectacular results.

This is a field of endeavour which the new government of China has been actively encouraging and it is to be hoped that great advances will be made. Outside scholars eagerly await the publication of finds that have been announced such as those at Ch'ang-sha on the middle Yangtze, dating apparently from the Warring States period (5th to 3rd centuries B.C.).

Primary documents in the narrower sense of written materials also exist in abundance, though sporadically. The earliest of these, the bone and shell fragments from the Shang dynasty have already been mentioned. Inscriptions on bronze vessels of the same and somewhat later periods are also important. Many inscriptions on stone exist, especially from the imperial period onward and since the art of taking rubbings has been practised for centuries many inscriptions valued for their calligraphic beauty or their historical references have been preserved even when the original stone is gone. Large collections of inscriptions have been printed. In recent times very many tomb inscriptions and the like which were not interesting enough to attract the attention of earlier collectors have been collected and preserved in Chinese museums. Unfortunately they are for the most part still unpublished.

The dry climate of north-west China and Turkestan has preserved documents on wood, silk and paper and as a result epoch-making discoveries have been made since the last decade of the 19th century. The most spectacular was the the opening of a hoard of manuscripts at Tun-huang dating from the 5th to the 11th century A.D. Apart from their interest for other fields of Chinese and Central Asian studies, they include unique examples of administrative and legal documents which are of the greatest importance for Chinese history.

Coming to later times, we find that original manuscripts are less rare, though still not common. The opening up of the Ch'ing imperial archives at the beginning of the republic released a very great deal of material, some of it dating back to Ming times. The archives of provincial and local govern-ments must have contained an immense amount of material as well but one's impression is that there has been little attempt to preserve it.

This enormous mass of source material presents a formidable task to the sinologists, especially to the few occidental sinologists who must first master the difficulties of the Chinese written language and then also often face acute problems of non-availability of essential material in the libraries where they work. It means *a fortiori* that there can be no question within the foreseeable future of providing the western general historian with an adequate body of translated sources for Chinese history.

Something has been done for the classical Chou period and the following Han, for which there is only a relatively restricted body of extant material. The main Confucian classics, including the so-called Book of History and the annals of the state of Lu, known as the Ch'un-ch'iu, together with the Tso-chuan, the more extensive chronicle attached to them as a commentary, have been translated, some of them more than once. So have some of the philosophic works not recognised as classics. A good deal of the first two standard histories has been rendered into French or English. The textual and linguistic difficulties of all this material are such however that the non-specialist must beware of attempting to base historical conclusions on them while the philological problems remain unsolved.

For later times questions of dating and authenticity are less vexing but the material is much vaster and, though there is certainly something to be said for translating certain very important texts, a serious researcher will obviously insist on supplementing them with the rest of the material in Chinese. Moreover, even to provide a translation of a historical text written in reasonably easy Chinese is no simple matter, for one is constantly beset by the problem of the rendering of terms whose meaning can only be adequately understood in their context in Chinese society. In short, the general historian must look to the sinologist not merely to provide him with raw material but to be a historian himself and to turn out a finished product comparable in standard to histories written about other parts of the world.

If we now turn to look at what has been done in the past by way of thus interpreting and presenting Chinese history to the west, we must be struck by the meagreness of the achievement in comparison with the immensity of the task.   How can one cavil at absurdities about China in general histories when scarcely less absurd errors disfigure the histories of China written by specialists ?   How can one expect appreciation of the complexities of Chinese civilisation when specialists so often continue to serve up a stale diet of clichés ?   To be sure the specialists are not to blame that they are too few and that China is too vast a subject to be comprehended by their feeble means.   Yet the fact remains that the task—surely an important one is not being accomplished.   What is the answer ?   More scholars ? More facilities ? Assuredly there is much that could be done in both these directions but it would be idle and out of place here to speculate on what one might hope for in that regard.   Yet it may be permissible to make one or two suggestions from one's personal point of view about the better use of the forces already at our disposal.

Firstly, we should surely be more aware of our duty to general historical studies as well as to our own specialities and try to present our ideas in a form useful to the non-specialist.   We should read other oriental history and non-oriental history and turn our attention to aspects of our own subject that have a wider interest; or illuminate our special problems from outside so that they in turn throw light on happenings in other times and places.   Secondly we should pay more attention to the results obtained by present-day Chinese and Japanese scholars.   I mention Japanese sinology in particular because it is so often neglected in the west.   I certainly do not believe that the job of western sinological studies should be confined to translating the results of Far Eastern scholarship but when one considers not only the initial advantages of familiarity with the Chinese character and infinitely better library facilities but also the vastly greater number of scholars engaged in studying Chinese history in the Far East, it is obviously disastrous to ignore their work.   By using their results, with due care and criticism, we can to some degree make up for the lack of a tradition of Chinese scholarship in the west comparable in solidity even to that in other branches of orientalism, let alone to that in classical or European historical studies.

In conclusion, we must ask the general historian to see our difficulties and be patient with our shortcomings, but not to ignore us or fail to recognise the importance of our studies to himself.

Bibliographical Note

An exhaustive bibliography of occidental literature on China up to the end of the second decade of the present century is provided by Henri Cordier, *Bibliotheca Sinica*, revised edition, I–IV (Paris, 1904–1908), *Supplément et Index* (Paris, 1922–24). Reprint available. This may be supplemented by Tung-li Yuan, *China in Western Literature* (New Haven, Yale University Far Eastern Publications, 1958), dealing with books in English, French, and German published between 1921 and 1957. *Tōyōshi kenkyū bunken ruimoku*, published serially since 1935 by Kyoto University, provides a systematic bibliography for Far Eastern History (excluding Japan), including works in western languages as well as in Chinese and Japanese. Charles O. Hucker, *China: A Critical Bibliography* (The University of Arizona Press, 1962), provides a very useful annotated list of recent and authoritative books and articles, mainly in English, designed for the use of American college students. Further, one may refer to the annual *Bibliography of Asian Studies*, published since 1956 by the *Journal of Asian Studies*, formerly the *Far Eastern Quarterly*; and to the *Revue bibliographique de sinologie* (years 1955–1960 so far covered), etc.

The most detailed account of Chinese history yet published in a Western language is Otto Franke, *Geschichte des Chinesischen Reiches*, I–V (Berlin, 1930–52), which stops at the beginning of the Ming dynasty. There are several shorter histories of varying merits, among which one may mention Edwin O. Reischauer and John K. Fairbank, *A History of East Asian Civilization*, I. *East Asia, The Great Tradition*, II. (with Albert M. Craig), *East Asia, The Modern Transformation* (Boston, Houghton Mifflin, 1960–65); Kenneth Scott Latourette, *The Chinese, their History and Culture*, 4th edition, two volumes in one (New York, Macmillan, 1964); L. Carrington Goodrich, *A Short History of the Chinese People*, 3rd edition (New York, Harper and Row, 1959; Harper Torchbook, 1963); René

Grousset, *Histoire de l'Extrême-Orient*, I–II (Paris, Geuthner, 1929); Wolfram Eberhard, *A History of China*, revised edition (University of California Press, 1960). The *Tōyō rekishi daijiten*, I–IX, new edition (Tokyo, 1951–54) gives a good account of the results of Japanese sinology to the date of publication. The more recent *Sekai rekishi jiten*, I–XXI (Tokyo, 1951–54), partially supplements it, but devotes considerably less space to the Far East.

A very important contribution to our knowledge of how Chinese observational science and technological inventiveness have influenced the rest of the world is provided by Joseph Needham, *Science and Civilization in China*, of which so far four volumes have appeared (Cambridge University Press, 1954–65) of a projected seven.

CENTRAL EURASIA

THE solid crust of the Earth forms only a thin layer on the surface of its total mass. Under this frail cover which men call their home and on which they build, the greater part by far of our globe is contained under tremendous pressure and heat. From time to time, fire erupts to the surface. The burning lava pours out, destroying and annihilating what man has built, bringing death and stillness to what before was life and movement. After a while the volcano subsides. The destroyed countryside revives, or else remains barren and lifeless for ever. A volcano does not build. It can only destroy, but the destruction coincides with its own death. The molten lava cools down. The flow ceases and all that remains of the beautiful, terrifying and impressive eruption is blackish-grey dust.

When we unfold before our eyes the map of Eurasia, this largest of all continents, we see that the great achievements of humanity, the main centres of civilisation, lie on its edges. Europe, the Semitic civilisation, Iran, India and China cover the shores of this immense island; only the northern shore, inaccessible to man because of its climate, has not produced its own major civilisation. Surrounded by this 'crust' of civilisation lie the immense wastes of Central Eurasia, little known, and unpredictable in their reactions—the Magma, the molten core around which most of world history has been built. When it comes to the surface, when it breaks through the shell within which the sedentary civilisations endeavour to contain it, man, horror-stricken, speaks of catastrophe. The forces of Hell have been let loose, God wishes to punish the world for its sins. And when the eruption calms down—as all eruptions must—the molten lava is added to the crust and helps to contain the forces that brought it to the surface. The solid crust becomes thicker and thicker. The eruptions become less frequent. The fire burns low and is less obvious. One tends almost to forget its existence.

Central Eurasian history cannot be located in time. It has existed ever since the history of the sedentary civilisations began. It is a necessary corrolary; it does not exist *per se*, but came into being only because the others existed, and side by side with them. There is no such thing as an absolute barbarian. He is an entity which can be defined only by comparison: the Brother of the Civilised, of the same blood but the Unsuccessful. They are opposed and complementary; interdependent, they constitute the proper order of this world. "Inside are those who don the cap and the girdle (the Chinese), outside are the barbarians" says the Chinese historian, to indicate that everything is in order, everybody in his proper place. Those who are outside attack, those who are inside resist. But only the centre of the civilised world is forbidden to the barbarian. He can, if he wishes, have access to the periphery and form a marginal group in the hope of being assimilated ultimately into the core. On the edges of civilisation a regular deposit of barbarian layers both increases constantly the area of the civilised world, and forms a protective reef around the initial centres. Thus the Hungarians who in the 11th century occupied their present country, then lying on the edges of European civilisation, became its most ardent defenders against invaders.

Only the less successful barbarian will content himself, however, with remaining on the periphery. His aim will normally be the complete conquest of the nearest and richest neighbour, and the replacement of its ruling class by himself. Once in possession of the coveted country, the Barbarian ceases to be what he has been. He is now on the other side of the fence and defends his new acquisition against the attack of fresh waves of Barbarians. The "Chinese" dynasty of Liao (907–1125 A.D.) was originally a small Mongol-speaking tribe of the northern Barbarians, the Kitans. During their reign in China their chief enemy was another tribe from Manchuria, the Tunguz-speaking Juchen. When the latter succeeded in ousting the Kitans from China and in themselves forming a "Chinese" dynasty (Chin 1125–1234,) the remnants of the Liao ruling class returned to Central Asia, where they succeeded in forming a flourishing nomad state.

This is, however, a rare phenomenon, the barbarian who has turned civilised usually prefers to lose his identity rather than to return to his former state. Even the Liao-Kitan example does not, strictly speaking, form an exception, for it is very likely that the mass of the Kitans preferred to remain in China, and that only a small group set out to re-make their fortunes in Central Asia. The Uigurs who in the 8th and and 9th centuries formed a powerful nomad empire in Mongolia, settled, when they were driven out, in the Chinese province of Kansu, and politely declined less than 100 years later an offer from the first Liao emperor to reinstate them in their former empire.

Historical circumstances may force a human group to remain in or to return to barbarism, but it never does so of its own free will. Who would like to leave the flesh pots and go forth into the wilderness? There are no volunteers for the Outer Darkness. To be a barbarian is a moral as well as an economic and political state. The history of Central Eurasia is a history of the barbarian.

*   *   *

The definition that can be given of Central Eurasia in space is negative. It is the part of the continent that lies beyond the borders of the great sedentary civilisations. This definition implies that this frontier is unstable. Although it varies from age to age, following the balance of pressure between the civilised and the uncivilised, it is easily traceable at any given moment of history.

One can imagine a time when the whole Eurasian continent belonged broadly to the same level of culture. However, such a theory is purely speculative. With the development of the great sedentary, agricultural civilisations the distinction between barbarian and civilised would have become for the first time marked. Although the area of Central Eurasia is subject to fluctuations, the general trend is that of diminution. With the territorial growth of the sedentary civilisations their borderline extends and offers a greater front to the depositing of Barbarian layers. The diminution in Space of Central Eurasia thus follows the pattern of a geometric progression;

as time goes on the process of assimilation becomes more and more rapid, in the sense that more and more barbarians can be assimilated within the same span of time. One would be inclined to expect a complete levelling if such an assumption would not imply a basic change in the world-pattern, a change that would resolve the timeless opposition between him who has and him who has not.

The Empires which were formed in Central Eurasia have been called the Empires of the Steppes: a beautiful and evocative term, worthy of Grousset, the scholar who coined it. It is not, however, entirely accurate. Central Eurasia consists not only of the Steppes but of the Taïga, the deep, coniferous forests, of limitless deserts and in the north, of the Tundra, the marches which have preserved in their eternally frozen and undisturbed depths the remains of the mammoth, chased there by creatures weaker, but more adaptable.

It is of course impossible to speak of uniform natural conditions in a territory which is four times larger than Europe; but it can safely be said that nature, far from being an ally, is there the most obstinate opponent of any human development. The relief may vary from place to place—lofty mountains or grassy plains may give a variety to the landscape; but the whole has to face the hardships of a rigorous continental climate with extreme cold and heat. In the region of the Altai Mountains, where lies the centre of most of the nomad Empires, for about 200 days in the year the temperature is below freezing point, with an average of -20 to $-30°$ C. in January and an average of $+15$ to $+20°$ C. in July. In the deserts east of the Caspian, and south of Lake Aral, where it freezes for between 30 and 90 days in the year, the average July temperature is between $+25$ and $+30°$ C. Such a climate forms a type of man who is incredibly tough, of an almost super-human endurance, adaptable, alert in mind but not devoted to metaphysical speculation.

Soil and climate are both unfavourable for agriculture, but large areas, as for instance the sub-alpine valleys of the Altai, are ideal grazing grounds, sufficient for the up-keep of hundreds of thousands of animals. Cattle breeding on a huge scale necessarily involves nomadism. The standard sentence of

Chinese historians when they speak of the "Barbarians of the West", is that "they follow their herds and the water." Indeed, a great part of the events that make up Central Eurasian history is determined by the necessity to provide food for the herds. The herds, then, in their turn, provide man with almost all that he needs for his food, clothes, housing, and, above all, in the case of horses, with a weapon that for thousands of years, ensured military superiority for the owner. When the Mongol troops stood on the coast of the Adriatic, they were unable to dispose of all their forces through lack of grass. Cities, fortified places, anything enclosed, are of no advantage to the Nomad. He cannot really grasp their true significance, and finds them cumbersome and useless. In the 13th century an ultimatum was addressed to Béla IV, king of Hungary, enjoining and also advising him to hand over to the Mongols the Comans, a nomad tribe which had taken refuge in Hungary; for—so the ultimatum goes—"it is easier for them to escape than for you (king of Hungary), since they, continually wandering in tents, may possibly escape, but you, living in houses, possessing fortresses and cities, how can you flee out of my grasp?" How significant these words are! How well they show the basic distrust of the Nomad for walls, which, so he feels, enclose more than they protect. So, the mobile felt tent becomes something more than one of the characteristic features of his civilisation, it becomes a symbol of the destiny shared by all those who "live under the felt tent."

It would nevertheless be wrong to imagine that all the inhabitants of Central Eurasia were nomads. The nomads were only the most successful among the barbarians, those who adopted a way of life likely to provide the greatest wealth. This did not come about without a fierce struggle, for as a basic condition they had to secure for themselves the grazing lands. The cattle breeder cannot live in the forest, and the forest-dweller's livelihood is provided by hunting. The relation of the forest-dweller to the cattle-breeder of the steppe can be compared to that existing between the latter and the sedentary peoples; the hunter is the unsuccessful, the barbarian who either did not succeed in conquering the necessary grazing grounds or who was chased away from them.

Time and again our sources speak of these peoples, hardly known to the sedentary, scattered in their forests, unconquerable, hunting the wild beasts on skis. If they are difficult to conquer it is mainly because they are elusive, and not because they are strongly organised. A hunter needs much space to provide him with the necessities of life, he is essentially an individualist, not likely to be a member of strongly organised communities. The basis of their economy being different, the hunters form an entity quite distinct from pastoral communities, and "people of the forest" is a generic term much in use, e.g. by the Mongols themselves.

More than once, some of the forest-people seem to have had some connection with metallurgy; and the knowledge of the art of working metals appears to have given them a power of which they made full use for political purposes. It is common to find that the monopoly of a trade or industry was used to obtain political advantages. The way to power always led, nevertheless, through pastoral nomadism, firstly because it was in itself the most productive and developed form of economy, secondly because it was the only economic structure capable of supporting a strong army.

When we consider both the natural circumstances of their setting, which precluded the possibility of agriculture on a large scale, and also the techniques of production of any epoch before the modern era, we can see that it was impossible for the peoples of Central Eurasia to devise any new means of production. Having reached in cattle-breeding the highest level attainable by the given means, they found their existence still precarious, and a particularly severe winter could bring about the complete economical, if not physical annihilation of the community. It is thus small wonder that the cattle-breeding communities made ample use of their military superiority, determined by their horse-breeding, to obtain goods beyond the reach of their own production. Thus, in its most developed form, the society of Central Eurasia is essentially predatory, and a basic opposition to sedentary civilisations remains its most distinctive feature. Economic production is limited to the supply of everyday needs and the surplus is looked for from booty and ransom.

Only to reach the highest stage of its evolution does the society of Central Eurasia need strong, centralised leadership. In peace time it is essential for the distribution of grazing land, for the smooth completion of the moving of the herds; in war the need for strong leadership is even more obvious, in fact it becomes a necessary condition of any systematic warfare. The way to leadership is very hard and few of those who attempted it reached their goal. Even fewer are those whose names history has recorded. First, followers must be gained one by one, and only when the initial expeditions have been successful does the movement achieve its own impetus.

The inscriptions of the Orkhon describe this process with poignancy. "My father, the Kaghan, went out with twenty-seven men. On hearing the rumour that he was going out and advancing, those who were in the towns went up into the mountains and those who were in the mountains came down, and when they were united they numbered 70. As Heaven gave them strength, my father's army was like a pack of wolves and his enemies were like sheep. Making war to the East and to the West, he gathered the people and made them rise and the number became 700. . . . He led in forty-seven campaigns and fought in twenty battles . . . and then he died. . . . My uncle came to the throne . . . and he made the poor, rich, and the few, numerous . . . the slaves became slave-owners and the serfs became owners of serfs. By the grace of Heaven and because I was lucky, I, myself, became a Kaghan and, having become Kaghan, I raised the poor and insignificant people. The poor I made rich; the few I made many."

The dislocation of such empires is even more rapid than their formation. When the leadership of the ruling class, i.e. the clan of the chief, ceases to be advantageous for the majority, the political framework will disintegrate and the empire cease to exist. Such political disappearances do not necessarily spell the complete annihilation of the people concerned. The individual either returns to a less prosperous way of life or, simply, pledges his allegiance to a new master. A victorious chief will have no difficulty in finding followers, only too glad to seize the opportunity of the greater prosperity he offers them. Growing numbers means growing power, increase in power and increase in wealth are synonymous. Up to the invention of fire-arms, which then gave the sedentary a decisive and permanent advantage, a pastoral nomad empire was practically invincible—as long as it remained united. "Because the younger brothers plotted against the elder brothers, because the nobles were quarrelling with the people : the Turk people brought about the ruin of its Kaghan who had reigned over it" lament the Orkhon inscriptions. This fact was well-known to all those such as the Chinese or Byzantines who had protracted dealings with barbarians. The precept *divide et impera* had a particular validity in Central Eurasia.

The characteristics of Central Eurasian history did not change in the course of time. Scythians or Mongols, Avars or Huns, they all followed the same pattern and are hardly distinguishable from one another. To revert to our initial image, the glowing magma burning under the tremendous pressure of the earth's solid crust is inarticulate. Its exact chemical substance can be determined only by complicated analysis, the differences inside the glowing mass are invisible to the naked eye. Closed in by walls—symbolic as those of Gog and Magog, or real as the one built by the Chinese—the barbarians fused into one great unity, in which national, religious or indeed linguistic differences are comparatively unimportant. So far as we can follow history, the course of evolution in Central Eurasia is not divergent but convergent, even the languages showing a slow process of equalisation. If there is a basic distinction made between man and man in the history of Central Eurasia, its criterion is social and economic rather than national or linguistic.

*   *   *

I should now like to consider the nature of the particular achievements of Central Eurasia. The question at once arises as to whether a people, *per definitionem* opposed to civilisation, living in great poverty, engaged in continual wars; a people whose political achievements were ephemeral; as to whether such a people could have produced anything of lasting value for humanity.

In art the achievements of Central Eurasia are very modest. I am aware that experts dealing with what is called the "art of the northern nomads" may find this judgment harsh. The graceful representations of the animal style, however great the delight they give us, are, after all, but minor achievements when compared with European, Chinese or Indian art. But, even if they had the same intrinsic value, this contribution of the nomads would be to but one of the arts through which men have sought for beauty. Architecture and sculpture were, by their very nature, beyond the reach of the Nomads. What genius they possessed went into the decoration of everyday utensils and commodities, easily moveable in their wanderings.

In the field of literature, the situation is hardly more favourable. We can enjoy the strength and vigour, and indeed the tenderness of some passages of the Orkhon inscriptions or of the Secret History of the Mongols, but the bulk of their written literature was imported, particularly in Buddhist texts.

Oral poetry was widely cultivated, but is for the most part lost, and presumably amounted to little when compared with the literatures of the great sedentary civilisations.

None of the great conquering religions originated in Central Eurasia, but this does not mean any lack of religious beliefs. Shamanism is a characteristic product of Central Eurasia. But what is Shamanism? In the forms in which it is known to the modern ethnographer it has ceased to be a system, and is very often nothing more than a chain of superstitious beliefs. But it is as if an ethnographer had no other sources for the study of Christianity than the practices of two or three hundred men belonging to different races and calling themselves Christians. The absence of written sources is, once more, the greatest obstacle in the way of research.

One must bear in mind when speaking of the religious achievements of Central Eurasia, that their mythology, which they have preserved but incompletely through lack of writing, has survived in other civilisations. China and Greece claim as their own, mythological themes which in fact originated in

Central Eurasia; and some of the striking correspondences which we can discover between the spiritual heritages of East and West are not due to late borrowings, or to the uniformity of the human mind. In more than one instance the explanation lies in the fact that both derive from a common source. I do not think that any of these great civilisations "borrowed" features from the religious systems of Central Eurasia, in the strict sense of this word. What I suggest, and what can be proved in a few cases, is that we can trace in their mythology remains of an epoch when no distinction existed between the civilised and the un-civilised. In mythology more than in anything else, the lurking Barbarian may be traced centuries after his imprints have vanished elsewhere.

Thus it can be said that in the religious field the spirit of Central Eurasia can boast of remarkable achievements. In one sense it is perhaps an achievement in itself that it gave birth to none of the conquering religions. Central Eurasia is remarkable for its religious tolerance. In the court of Möngke, Buddhists, Taoists and all sorts of Christian sects were represented and lived peacefully together. Peacefully because the great Khan would not have tolerated them otherwise.

The question of religious tolerance takes us one step further, and leads us to examine the characteristics of the political achievements of Central Eurasia. We use the expression political in the widest possible sense, as the ordering of human relations, both within and without the same community.

The organisation of such immense territories as were usually under the rule of a Nomadic Empire, would have been impossible without some sort of collaboration from the local populations. As long as the expansion did not extend across sedentary civilisations, this was a comparatively easy task, for the peoples of Central Eurasia themselves were ready to accept the leadership of a successful man likely to provide them with improved conditions. The religious tolerance, the general un-nationalistic approach where even differing languages seem not to have constituted any major obstacle, facilitated the quick integration of various elements in a common aim. This aim was conquest: the only practicable way to improve economic conditions. War, as waged by the barbarians, was a horrible and ruthless undertaking. It was no more cruel in its methods, however, than that waged by the civilised; and it was more successful. Cruelty is seldom to be found among the peoples of Central Eurasia. None of their absolute monarchs, in whose hands rested immense, almost unlimited, power, ever indulged in cruel amusements so common among Roman and Chinese emperors. Mongols killed the enemy but only the enemy, and only as long as it seemed purposeful. Attila, "The Scourge of God", was a harmless person compared with Nero or Caligula, and he was loved by his people. Even at the height of their powers, even divinised and served with a most rigid etiquette, these rulers did not lose their simplicity. They lived with their people, were accessible to them and did their best "to make the poor people rich." The Greek Priscus at Attila's court, and the Franciscan monks at the Mongol court were all struck by the dignity of these monarchs and by the efficiency and the smoothness with which their huge empires were administered.

As war was the main source of income to barbarians, they had to do all they could to ensure its successful outcome. Throughout centuries a strategy was evolved that we cannot but admire. No one ever made better use of cavalry than the people of Central Eurasia. Not only did they produce a strain of horse eminently suited to their purposes, but they also invented the stirrup which opened new horizons for the use of horses. With constant and systematic training begun in early childhood, they achieved a skill in riding and shooting with bows from horseback that has remained un-paralleled. Everything was directed to the perfecting of military techniques and even the Chinese, in the 3rd century B.C., had to adopt, much to their displeasure, the costume of the Nomads, so suitable for warfare. Over and above the individual skill of the soldier, in Central Eurasia, stands a highly perfected strategy: a real art in the highest form of warfare, which, it can be said without exaggeration, was only equalled in the second World War. Mongol conquests were a result of what we, today, should call "logistical warfare." One is greatly impressed by the sight of different army-corps, separated by thousands of miles, operating independently but under a single command, and co-ordinating their movements so as to meet on a given day and at a given place. Everything was organised and foreseen, everything calculated. The perfectly trained troops resisted even the temptation to loot in order to obey orders. I think that the greatest achievement of Central Eurasia lies in the fact that it produced a spirit of solidarity; a spirit of discipline and self-denial that is seldom, if ever, equalled in world history. The leaders of Central Eurasian peoples were past-masters in the management of huge human groups. It is a pity that these qualities were not, could not be, used for more constructive purposes. The techniques of the time did not make it possible to augment economic production and to improve the welfare of their peoples in the hard conditions of Central Eurasia, except by conquest.

*   *   *

If we try to detect those features of Central Eurasian history which were the most important from the point of view of general history, the main point is the rôle of this area as an intermediary between the great sedentary civilisations on which it bordered.

Although as a rule the huge nomad empires did not cover the whole of Central Eurasia, the expanse of a number of them was so considerable as to be limitrophe to more than one of the sedentary civilisations; and those parts of Central Eurasia which were nominally not dependent on such an empire were not sufficiently organised politically to prevent communication taking place across them. The nomads carried the art of the Greeks, of Transcaucasia or of the Iranians across the wastes of Siberia to China, and they amalgamated into one art motives taken up at random. To quote the eminent archaeologist Sir Ellis Minns, "It is not therefore pure coincidence that a brick from a Chinese tomb of the Wei Dynasty should oddly resemble the familiar Viking relief from St. Paul's Churchyard in London."

Not only art motives were carried through Central Eurasia, but also goods of all sorts. The great Silk Road, of which mention has been made elsewhere in this book, led for its greater part through territories under the control of barbarians. Whenever a great nomad state flourished, bringing with it improved conditions of travel, the traffic between China and India, Iran and the Western world became brisker.

The spirit of tolerance that permeated the nomad states made them particularly open to religious influences. Buddhism, Manchaeism, Zoroastrianism reached China through Central Asia, and so did Christianity. Some of these religions left but little imprint on China, others, particularly Buddhism, were more influential. It is interesting to note that whereas commerce and techniques followed in the main an East-to-West direction, in things of the spirit a West-to-East trend can be observed. Indian or Chinese thought left no trace in the West, whereas Iranian, Indian and Christian religions played an infinitely greater rôle in the Far East. I think that this should be ascribed to the fact that Central Eurasia acted as an intermediary. Whatever the extension of the greatest nomad states may have been, their centre lay in Mongolia and their chief interest focused on China. As everywhere, it was the court of the ruler that became a centre of intellectual activity; and as these courts were in China's neighbourhood rather than in the Occident, priests and missionaries had to travel from the western marches of a nomad empire right to the Far East to be presented to the ruler. So Franciscans had to go to Karakorum in Mongolia in order to meet the great khan, whereas there was nobody on the western parts of Central Eurasia to whom a Taoist monk would have wished to travel.

The location of the ruler's court also led to the presence of numbers of Europeans or Iranian prisoners and "displaced persons" in Mongolia and China. It is often forgotten that in the 13th century an imperial guard was formed in China from Alans, native in the Caucasus, and that a Russian colony existed then in North China.

As for the transmission from East to West of technical achievements, such as the manufacture of silk, or printing, I should rather suppose that it was the Europeans who were instrumental in their spread. There is no doubt that the spirit of adventure which has carried white men to the furthest ends of the globe is almost their monopoly. Europe can boast of having produced the greatest discoverers and travellers, although as far as Central Eurasia is concerned only very few of those who first travelled through it are known to us by name, and even fewer have left a written record of their experiences. The achievements of the great 13th century travellers, Plano Carpini, Rubruck, Marco Polo and the others, awake our profound admiration, but it appears from their accounts that dozens of other Europeans preceded them to Mongolia, and some of those who returned must have brought back the knowledge of Chinese techniques. Marco Polo's written account helps us to assess the amount of information which must have been transmitted verbally by him and others.

Although the transmission of technological inventions may have been the achievement of Europeans, it was made possible through the organisation of the great nomad empires.

It is more difficult to assess other aspects of Central Eurasia's main contribution to general history. Among these, one can note that throughout the ages, the barbarians remained the principal enemies of China, and it would be difficult to imagine what turn Chinese history would have taken without their pressure. In the Christian era alone, China was for about 800 years under the rule of barbarian dynasties.

Successive incursions into Europe, such as those made by the Huns, Avars and Hungarians, were an important factor in their own times; but among all the barbarian states the Mongol empire left the most indelible trace on human history. From this general point of view the Mongol rule over China is perhaps not as significant as its influence on the destinies of the Middle East. The devastation of Persia and Khorezm, which never recovered from this destruction, the sack of Baghdad and the murder of the Caliph are major events on any scale. The impact of the Mongols on Russia was considerable and among other features characteristic of this country, the development of an autocratic tradition must be considered as one of the results of Mongol occupation. Until modern times no state ever reached the extension of that of the Mongols. Directly or indirectly it left a deep imprint on general history.   *   *   *

The study of Central Eurasia presents difficulties of a peculiar nature. Almost all of them go back to the lack of aboriginal sources. These peoples, who were, historically speaking, so incredibly active, had small feeling for historical tradition, and each of the successive empires was too short-lived for the establishment of a deep-rooted tradition. But this is, strictly speaking, only the pyschological reason for the absence of written sources. There is another reason, material this time, and more important. The art of writing was not widespread among the barbarians, and the chances of survival for the few written documents, in a society constantly on the move and without permanent settlements, were slender indeed. It must be said, however, that the monuments of native history which have come down to us are of exceptional value. They are important not only because they are rare, but also because of their particular beauty, and because they give us a splendid insight into the formation and functioning of nomadic empires. Two monuments merit particular attention : the Turkish inscriptions found near the river Orkhon, dating from the 8th century A.D., and the Secret History of the Mongols from the 13th century A.D., written in Mongol. It is significant in itself that not one single indigenous document has come down to us to shed any light on the 500 years or so that elapsed in between. The curious thing is, too, that the writers of the second document had no knowledge of the epoch in which the first inscriptions have to be placed. Another people had written their own history in another language. When one reads both, however, when one penetrates into their spirit, one cannot help but realise the timeless uniformity of the history of the barbarians.

The few aboriginal sources we do have at our disposal are not easy to handle. The inscriptions of the Orkhon were engraved in a script that had to be deciphered in order to discover their contents. As they are the longest documents written in this script, almost no external help comes to the rescue of the philologist, and a number of obscure passages will, it is to be feared, remain for ever obscure. The reading of the Secret History of the Mongols places before the philologist a difficult task indeed. The text is one of the earliest documents in Mongol and presents characteristics which cannot be found in any of the better-known Mongol languages. But what makes the reading of this chronicle even more difficult is the curious form in which it has been preserved. The Mongol text came down to us in Chinese transcription, that is, the polysyllabic Mongol language was transcribed as well as possible into Chinese monosyllables. As we do not know the exact phonetic value of 13th-century Chinese characters, and as we did not know until the discovery of the Secret History the pronunciation of 13th-century Mongol, the reconstruction of the original presented considerable difficulty. A number of the difficulties are still unsolved, but as they are philological they do not detract from the historical usefulness of the text, which thus constitutes the main source of Mongol history, and, indeed, the most revealing written source of Central Eurasia.

We thus have at our disposal, over a period of some two thousand years for the whole of Central Eurasia, only these two major, original historical sources. All the rest that we know we owe to sources written by the sedentary peoples who surrounded Central Eurasia. This puts the historian in a very difficult position. It is easy to visualise the difficulties he has to face when he sets himself the task of reconstructing history, having at his disposal exclusively hostile information. But what makes the task of the historian even more complicated is the necessity for him to penetrate into the mysteries of Chinese or Persian philology in order to solve his problems. For his work of writing history, he has to rely on Chinese, Islamic and Greek sources, to mention only three main groups. Occasionally, even, he has to tackle Slavonic material and medieval Latin. If he is not an expert in each of these fields— and who can claim to be one!—he has to rely on second-hand information, which is, in most cases, utterly inadequate to provide him with the solid basis on which he can build. Another part of this book shows the difficulties of handling Chinese material. As reliable translations are very rare, each little mosaic stone brought into the picture must be hammered into place with hard work. The handling of Persian sources is slightly easier, but even here the difficulties are so great that a historian trained in dealing with European sources finds it difficult even to conceive of the problems entailed. The main advantage when compared with the Chinese material is the smaller quantity of the Persian material. It is also very often more colourful and less schematic. A danger lies in the lack of originality. Information several centuries old is given as contemporary. Works are copied and copied again, without any regard for the reality of what may or may not lie behind them. This element is not entirely absent from Byzantine sources. Here the literary exigencies, the desire to make the work conform to some classic, distorts the truth and leads to anachronisms not always easy to detect. But at least Byzantine historians are European, they are our ancestors and their ways of thinking are not only more comprehensible to us but are, on the whole, more critical. A different light falls on events from Chinese, Persian and European sources. Although this has obvious advantages, the effects of light and shade thus achieved make it hard to recognise the same fact when described by different methods. This difficulty becomes particularly apparent in connection with proper names.

The Turkish or Mongol proper name transcribed by a Chinese or Persian historian, to whom it was previously unknown, becomes, quite often, unrecognisable. This is not only due to initial carelessness on the part of the historian, but also to the inherent difficulty of transcribing a foreign name into Chinese characters or of rendering a foreign name in Arabic script. The difficulties involved in reading an old text written in this script are too well known to necessitate a detailed description here. Usually the context helps us to supply the missing elements and to make the necessary emendations, but when it comes to reconstructing a proper name in its original form and thus, very often, identifying the person to whom the events related refer, a satisfactory result can only be achieved, if at all, through considerable and detailed investigation. A glance at a number of European books on Mongol history will reveal such discrepancies between the spelling of proper names that the student will be tempted to ascribe deeds to two different persons which have been performed by one person only. The historian has to face difficulties of a rather primitive nature in the different European transcriptions of Chinese names (which in our case are in their turn transcriptions of other foreign names). He may find, in a European manual, the English transcription, for instance, of a Chinese word which, in 13th-century pronunciation (often differing from that of to-day) transcribes the Persian form of a European proper name. The longer the chain the easier the misunderstandings. For the non-orientalist historian, it must be an absolute rule never to base any hypothesis on the similarity between proper names as rendered in a European work. Ever since the 18th century the identification of the Hiung-nu with the Huns has haunted and still haunts our manuals, although the whole theory is in fact based on a vague similarity between the transcription of the two names.

The difficulties just mentioned are, on the whole, of a philological nature. They constitute only the first obstacle in the arduous journey of the historian. As I have said before, almost our entire documentation comes from sources alien to the people it describes. One shudders at the thought of what it would mean to write English history having as sole witness, for example, French and Indian sources, and the case is very often similar in Central Eurasian history. But, not only have we to reconstruct the original picture through the distorting mirror of alien interpretations, we are also compelled to supplement it.

Chinese or Byzantines were interested in barbarian history only in so far as their own political interests went. The name of a people appears in the Chinese sources only when it meant some trouble for the administration, and the remarks are mostly limited to an arid enumeration of incursions, victories and defeats. From time to time a particularly odd feature of their civilisation may have struck the imagination of a Chinese historian, and found its way into the annals of their history or into some encyclopaedia. For a historian used to an abundance of written sources, it might be astonishing to see with what scanty material the historian of Central Eurasia has to be content. The entire material that deals with the Turks, who formed one of the most important empires of

Central Eurasia and who were for some 200 years the most dangerous enemies of the ruling dynasty, if put into European book-form, would not amount to more than, say, 200 printed pages. The notice on their Western Empire included in the annals of the T'ang dynasty amounts to less than forty pages in the French translation.

Our knowledge of Central Eurasian history is, however, not entirely based on the evidence of written sources. Archaeology and linguistics have done more than a little to supplement the information we have, and they can even provide us with clues on matters on which written sources remain silent.

Owing to the peculiar character of Central Eurasian civilisation, archaeological findings are quantitatively unimportant if compared with almost any part of the Old World. The remains of civilisations that built no cities are necessarily perishable. Most of the findings are small objects in metal and only on very rare occasions has the frozen soil preserved organic materials; cloth and even human remains. Owing to the immensity of the territory involved and the extreme scarcity of the population, findings have been till now very rare, and we can confidently expect that future years will bring important archaeological discoveries.

Unfortunately, archaeological results are in our field seldom convertible into historical terms. It is always hazardous to attribute archaeological discoveries to a definite people. On what grounds, without outside evidence, can a tomb be ascribed to one people rather than to another? When one reads that such tombs belonged to a Turkish or Mongol people, one can hardly resist asking the facetious question as to whether the pot, the bow or indeed the skull found greeted its discoverer with a Turkish or Mongol sentence to facilitate the identification.

This brings us to the second question; the examination of the extent to which linguistics contribute to the study of Central Eurasia. The help that linguistics can offer is very little indeed, and can only be used to shed some light on proto- or pre-historical periods. The important thing again is of a rather negative nature : one should not ascribe a language to a people without definite information. It might be appropriate to recall, at this juncture, that in spite of what one can conclude from the reading of manuals, we do not know what languages, e.g., the Huns, the Avars, the Hsiung-nu and the Zhuan-zhuan spoke. When we speak of them as Turks and Mongols, we only beg the question.

In these circumstances, it would be idle to pretend that the results of historical investigations in this sphere can ever lay claim to the solidarity to which research in European history has accustomed us. This, however, does not mean that we have to abandon all the critical spirit without which reliable history cannot be written. It is depressing to realise to what extent this elementary precaution has been neglected. Historians have mostly overcome the philological difficulties in these historical studies by ignoring them. The innumerable books written, for example, on Chingis Khan, have rarely more solid foundation than three or four other European books written about him, and have little more original work in them than the personal 'interpretation' of the author—about as solid and penetrating as a sixth-form schoolboy could give on Julius Caesar. The question now arises as to whether, for instance, it is possible to write on Central Eurasian history at all with any degree of accuracy; as to whether it would not be better to concentrate on the translation of and commentary on all the sources available, and to abandon, anyhow for the time being, any attempt at synthesis. I do not think that such a view should necessarily be taken.

It is clearly essential that further material should be made available. It seems to me that this is particularly important as regards Islamic sources, which, to my mind, are likely to yield more important and more colourful material than we can expect from Chinese sources. It can also be hoped that as time goes by archaeological research will contribute more and more to our knowledge of Central Eurasia. The prospects in this field are immense. The same cannot be said of linguistic studies. It is very unlikely that any new or important discovery will be made, and so research will have to content itself with what material is available.

Analytical research, to be really efficient, needs some working hypothesis and so I should not like to advocate the abandonment of any attempt to synthesize. What is essential is that such work should be undertaken in a very critical spirit, should be based on all the available material and not on one or two facts, selected at random.

The recommendations one would like to make to orientalists interested in history are more negative than positive. It would be of more use if they were to set out less frequently to prove something and would content themselves with describing happenings. There is too great a tendency towards the sensational; towards the discovery, say, of some new, amazing migration. That this approach is not necessary has been proved by René Grousset, whose *Empire des Steppes** can serve as a perfect example of what can and should be done.

The first quality needed by the historian interested in Central Eurasia is distrust. The mirage of easy and unwarranted identification is perhaps the greatest danger. I mentioned earlier on that the historical identification of the Huns with the Hsiung-nu is based on a vague assonance between their names. Examples could easily be multiplied. Time and again one reads of Turks or Mongols in pre-Christian times, although the former appeared only in the 6th century, and the latter do not emerge before the 9th century (it would be wiser not to mention them until the 13th century). And when one examines the evidence that lies behind these statements, one finds such a wholly gratuitous remark as that the mythical peoples mentioned by Herodotus, the Arimaspoi for example, are Turks or Mongols. The Hyperborean mountains of the Greeks are identified with the Altai mountains or the Ural mountains, or the Himalayas, to suit the needs of any particular hypothesis. The people of the Tingling, for whom our entire material amounts only to a few pages in Chinese sources, containing very little information of any use, will happily be identified with the Samoyedes in book after book, simply on the strength of the fact that they are said to use skis. One is baffled by the lack of critical spirit that often prevails. Sciolism seems to follow the example of the barbarian himself, who, being excluded from hospitable

* Paris, 1939; 4th ed., 1952. The only book on Central Eurasia I can thoroughly recommend.

areas, takes refuge in Central Eurasia, perhaps the last of the happy hunting grounds of the dilettante historians.

By a pinch of scepticism one could have avoided most of the numerous blunders made in the study of Central Eurasia.

But there are difficulties where a critical spirit alone will not help and a thorough knowledge of bibliography is needed. Some years ago a most distinguished historian of religion made an extremely penetrating study of a Central Eurasian god. He gave a painstaking analysis of the passages where the god's name occurs in Turkish inscriptions, and did his best to fit him into the general picture. Alas! the god was but a mis-reading, corrected almost fifty years before in a most technical article which has nothing in its title to attract the interest of an historian of religion. It is a pity, for the god in question will probably haunt manuals of religious history for innumerable years to come.

Examples could be multiplied, but this may suffice. Synthesis, if it is to lay claim to accuracy, must be based on solid fact. Those who for one reason or another cannot check the validity of their basic material should abstain from dealing with Central Eurasian history. It is better not to know than to be mistaken, or, to quote Pelliot—who did more than anyone in this field to eradicate mistakes—"Une science probe doit se résoudre à beaucoup ignorer."

*   *   *

I have tried to fit Central Eurasia into the general framework of history and to indicate the problems peculiar to its study. Few fields of research are more promising for those who approach historical studies with the proper critical spirit and preparation. The effort needed is considerable, for no one can hope to grasp the problems of Central Eurasia without previously studying at least one or two of the surrounding civilisations. Labour will, however, be rewarded by a constant flow of discoveries, and a new world will open before him who is not afraid to work this unbroken ground. Students of Central Eurasia have to face the hardships and the satisfactions of pioneers. The harvest is indeed great, but the labourers are few.

Bibliographical Note

When the first edition of this work was prepared, the only history of Central Eurasia worth mentioning was that of René Grousset, *L'empire des steppes* (Paris, Payot, 1939, reprinted: 1948). While this excellent work is still of interest and use, it is a pleasure to record that since 1954 the study of Central Eurasian or, more loosely, Inner Asian, history has made spectacular progress.

The standard reference work, Denis Sinor, *Introduction à l'étude de l'Eurasie Centrale* (Wiesbaden, Otto Harrassowitz, 1963) contains hundreds of precise and pertinent bibliographical data.

It so happens that since the publication of that book several fairly comprehensive histories of Inner Asia have appeared: *Geschichte Mittelasiens*, in *Handbuch der Orientalistik*, vol. V, 5, edited by B. Spuler (Leiden-Köln, E. J. Brill, 1966); *Zentralasien*, edited by Gavin Hambly, vol. 16 of *Fischer Weltgeschichte* (Fischer Bücherei, Frankfurt-am-Main, 1966), both collective works. Denis Sinor, *Inner Asia. History—Civilization—Languages. A Syllabus* (Indiana University Publications, Uralic and Altaic Series, vol. 96, Bloomington and The Hague, 1969), which, as its title indicates, is basically a syllabus for a university course. Among these more comprehensive works should be mentioned the Очерки истории СССР of which the following two volumes are of particular interest to our studies: Крисиз рабовладельческой системы и зарождение феодализма на территории СССР, III–IX веков, edited by V. A. Rybakov (Moskva, 1958), and, edited by A. N. Nasonov, L. V. Čerepnin, and A. A. Zimin, Период феодализма конец XV в начало XVIII в (Moskva, 1955). Somewhat dated but still of use: W. Barthold, *12 Vorlesungen über die Geschichte der Türken Mittelasiens* (Berlin, 1935; reprint available. The French translation of this work is useless).

A special place is due to Owen Lattimore's pioneering works, viz. *Inner Asian Frontiers of China* (American Geographical Society Research Series, vol. 21, New York, 1940; paperback reprint: Beacon Press) and *Studies in Frontier History. Collected Papers 1928–1958* (Oxford University Press, 1962).

Research on the prehistory of Central Eurasia lies almost exclusively in Soviet hands. On the pertinent archaeological literature there is the excellent guide of N. A. Vinberg, T. N. Zadneprovskaja, and A. A. Ljubimova, Советская археологическая литература. Библиография 1941–1957 (Moskva and Leningrad, 1959). Much can be learned from A. L. Mongait, *Archaeology in the U.S.S.R.*, translated and adapted by M. W. Thompson (Pelican Book, 1961). The series Материалы и исследования по археологии СССР, published by the Archaeological Institute of the Soviet Academy, is an inexhaustible mine of information. So far more than a hundred and fifty volumes have appeared. They are not solely concerned with the study of prehistory; other periods open to archaeological investigation receive the same attention. The principal periodical in this field is Советская археология (published since 1936).

A thorough knowledge of Siberia, its past and present, is of great importance for the history of Central Eurasia. The collective work История Сибири с древнейших времен до наших дней greatly facilitates access to the basic facts and to the relevant literature. Of five volumes contemplated, four have so far been published (Leningrad, 1968). Народы Сибири, edited by M. G. Levin and L. P. Potapov (Moskva, 1956), gives a detailed and fascinating picture of the indigenous civilization. There is a slightly abridged but very useful English translation: *The Peoples of Siberia* (The University of Chicago Press, 1964).

There are but a handful of readable and yet reliable monographs devoted to a definite chapter of Central Eurasian history. Disregarding source editions, for the medieval period the following may be recommended: W. Barthold, *Turkestan down to the Mongol Invasion*, 2nd edition (London, E. J. W. Gibb Memorial Series, N.S.V., 1928); Édouard Chavannes, *Documents sur les Tou-kiue (Turcs) Occidentaux* (St. Pétersbourg, 1903; reprint available); D. M. Dunlop, *The History of the Jewish Khazars* (Princeton University Press, 1954); M. I. Artamonov, История Хазар (Leningrad, 1962); E. A. Thompson, *A History of Attila and the Huns* (Oxford University Press, 1948).

On the Mongol period: Bertold Spuler, *The Muslim World. A Historical Survey. Pt. II. The Mongol Period* (Leiden, E. J. Brill, 1960); *Die Goldene Horde. Die Mongolen in Russland*

1223–1502, 2nd edition (Wiesbaden, Otto Harrassowitz, 1965);
*Die Mongolen in Iran. Verwaltung und Kultur der Ilchanzeit
1220–1350* (Leipzig, 1939); *Geschichte der Mongolen.
Nach östlichen und europäischen Zeugnissen des 13. und 14. Jahrhunderts*
(Zürich, Artemis Verlag, 1968). The best biography of Chingis
is the English translation of René Grousset, *Le conquérant du
monde* (Paris, 1944) published under the title *Conqueror of the
World* (New York, The Orion Press, 1966; Edinburgh, Oliver
and Boyd, 1967). There is a complete and fairly accurate
German translation of the Secret History of the Mongols by
Erich Haenisch, *Die Geheime Geschichte der Mongolen. Aus einer
Niederschrift des Jahres 1240 von der Insel Kode'e im Keluren Fluss*,
2nd edition (Leipzig, 1948). Arthur Waley, *The Secret History
of the Mongols and other pieces* (London, Allen and Unwin, 1963)
contains a highly readable but only partial translation based
on the Chinese version of this important document. The
fascinating reports by the early missionaries to the Mongols are
among the best sources on Mongol civilization of the 13th
century. A readable translatión of the principal texts was
edited by Christopher Dawson, *Mission to Asia* (New York,
Harper Torchbooks, 1966). On the social organization of the
Mongols: B. Vladimirtsov, *Le régime social des Mongols. Le
féodalisme nomade* (Paris, Adrien-Maisonneuve, 1948); Valentin
A. Riasanovsky, *Fundamental Principles of Mongol Law* (Tientsin,
1937; Reprint: Indiana University Publications, Uralic and
Altaic Series, vol. 43, 1965).

Special mention should be made of Emanuel Sarkisyanz,
Geschichte der orientalischen Völker Russlands bis 1917 (München,
R. Oldenbourg, 1961). It contains data on almost all the
peoples of Central Eurasia in a form so condensed as to make
the book virtually unreadable. But Sarkisyanz's facts are
usually reliable and for the post-Mongol and modern periods—
for Turkestan, the Caucasus, Siberia, or the Volga region—his
book is by far the best general guide we have.

On the later Mongol khanates: I. J. Zlatkin, История
джунгарского ханства: 1635–1748 (Moskva, 1964); Maurice
Courant, *L'Asie Centrale aux XVII–XVIIIe siècles. Empire kalmouk
ou empire mantchoux* (Annales de l'Université de Lyon, N.S. 26,
1912). On modern Mongolia: C. R. Bawden, *The Modern*

History of Mongolia (London, Weidenfeld and Nicolson; New York, Frederick A. Praeger, 1968).

On early Russo-Mongol relations the magnificent volumes of John F. Baddeley, *Russia, Mongolia, China, I–II* (London, 1919; reprint available) will have to be supplemented by Paul Pelliot, *Notes critiques d'histoire kalmouke, I–II* (Paris, Adrien-Maisonneuve, 1960).

There is no dearth of works dealing with Turkestan of the post-Mongol period. For introductory reading on what is called Russian Central Asia one can recommend V. V. Barthold, *Four Studies on the History of Central Asia, I–III*, translated from the Russian by V. and T. Minorsky (Leiden, E. J. Brill, 1956–62). Most of the relevant literature is in Russian, e.g. P. P. Ivanov, Очерки по истории Средней Азии (XVI-середина XIX в.) (Moskva, 1958); S. E. Tolibekov, Общественно-экономический строй казаков в XVII–XIX веках (Alma-Ata, 1959); Ju. Ê. Bregel', Хорезмские туркмены в XIX веке (Moskva, 1961), etc.

There is a rich literature in English dealing with the last century or so of the history of Turkestan. These books tend to concentrate on the Russian rather than the Turkic aspects, and are often biased and superficial. The most serious among them are Seymour Becker, *Russia's Protectorates in Central Asia: Bukhara and Khiva, 1865–1924* (Harvard University Press, 1968) and on the same topic, Hélène Carrère d'Encausse, *Réforme et révolution chez les Musulmans de l'Empire Russe* (Cahiers de la Fondation Nationale des Sciences Politiques, 141, Paris, Armand Colin, 1966). The title of Geoffrey Wheeler, *The Modern History of Soviet Central Asia* (London, Weidenfeld and Nicolson; New York, Frederick A. Praeger, 1964) is misleading: almost one half of the book deals with the pre-Soviet period. The same remark can apply also to Olaf Caroe, *Soviet Empire. The Turks of Central Asia and Stalinism*, 2nd edition (London, Macmillan; New York, St. Martin's Press, 1967). In the following works emphasis is given to civilization and culture: Edward Allworth (editor), *Central Asia. A Century of Russian Rule* (Columbia University Press, 1967); Alexandre Bennigsen and Chantal Lemercier-Quelquejay, *Islam in the Soviet Union* (London, Pall Mall Press; New York, Frederick A. Praeger,

1967), a revised French edition: *L'Islam en Union Soviétique* (Paris, Payot, 1968); Elizabeth E. Bacon, *Central Asians under Russian Rule. A Study in Culture Change* (Cornell University Press, 1966). The bulk of the research on the spiritual and material culture of the peoples of Central Eurasia is published in the form of articles. The periodical Советская этнография (published since 1931) is particularly valuable from this point of view, although most of the articles deal with contemporary and near-contemporary topics. On beliefs concerning the supernatural one can recommend Uno Harva, *Die religiösen Vorstellungen der altaischen Völker* (Folklore-Fellows Communications, 125, Helsinki, 1938); V. Diószegi (editor), *Popular Beliefs and Folklore Tradition in Siberia* (Indiana University Publications, Uralic and Altaic Series, vol. 56, Bloomington and The Hague, 1968); Jean-Paul Roux, *Faune et flore sacrées dans les sociétés altaiques* (Paris, Adrien-Maisonneuve, 1966). On literature: Nora K. Chadwick and Victor Zhirmunsky, *Oral Epics of Central Asia* (Cambridge University Press, 1969).

It can hardly be over-emphasized: it is in articles rather than in books that the greatest contributions to Central Eurasian historiography have been made. The fact that the name of Paul Pelliot—perhaps the greatest scholar who has ever worked in this field—appears only once in this short bibliography is due to circumstances limiting bibliographical references to books. Relevant articles will be found dispersed in many periodicals focused on Asia and more specifically in *Ural-Altaische Jahrbücher* (since 1952, continuation of *Ungarische Jahrbücher*) and in *Central Asiatic Journal* (since 1955), both published by Otto Harrassowitz, Wiesbaden. Up to the death of Pelliot in 1945, the volumes of *T'oung Pao* (published by E. J. Brill, Leiden) contained scores of important articles on Central Eurasia.

The Cambridge History of Inner Asia, edited by Denis Sinor, now under active preparation, will attempt a synthesis on a hitherto unprecedented scale.

DENIS SINOR

EPILOGUE

I SHOULD like to bring this book to a close by a few personal remarks suggested by what has been said in the preceding chapters. I do not intend to give a full summary of the main results nor do I wish to introduce any considerations which could not be substantiated by the material expounded in the body of the book.

I find particularly interesting the way in which each author defined the area he was in charge of.

Clearly, each area discussed in this book has its own individuality; each of them shows a peculiar and different conjunction of characteristics, some of which may occur individually in other areas but all of which cannot be found combined in the same proportion elsewhere. Some of the constituents are common, some particular, and naturally constituents of the second category only can serve to distinguish one area from another. But constituents that are particular to one area, must necessarily be common to a certain number of smaller units, which in their turn are determined by constituents common only to them. This book deals with very large areas and, at the outset of our task, I was not certain that these corresponded in fact with historical realities, that all the peoples englobed within them had in fact common constituents. I think it can be asserted now, that my fears were unjustified, for each author found it quite natural to deal with the area assigned to him, and did not hesitate to define it, to indicate its border and, thereby, to distinguish it from areas lying beyond them.

It is tempting to investigate within each area the nature of those characteristics which form its common constituents. Our first conclusions will be negative.

(a) The political factor does not seem to play an important rôle. None of the five areas described coincides with any political unity. Either such unities are incorporated within an area—i.e. they present such common constituents as are characteristic of the whole of it—or else they straddle two or more areas.

(*b*) Racial distinction does not seem to have played any rôle in the forging of the great historical unities of Asia.

(*c*) None of the authors considered language as the main uniting link; with the exception perhaps of China, all the areas are multilingual.

What are then, in the view of the authors, those factors that determine, in space and time, the areas with which they are concerned? According to H. Frankfort, the Ancient Near East "Denotes the extent, in space and time, of the earliest civilised societies" (p. 1). It includes thus, within a given time, everything within its own purview that is not barbarian. The same criterion also applies, in another part of the world, to China. Pulleyblank's chapter shows clearly that the concept "China" is essentially one of civilisation symbolised mainly by the Chinese script. "All under Heaven" is Chinese, it is civilisation *par excellence*, the rest of the world being but barbarism. Central Eurasia is on the other side of the pale, it is barbarism *par excellence* as opposed to civilisation. The criteria to the definition of these three areas are essentially social, the *fundamentum divisionis* is the cultural and economical (relative) standard of the area but not its (absolute) content.

This is not so with the two remaining areas. The unity of Islam rests on the unity of faith, and, to quote van Lohuizen (p. 36), "India's unity lay not so much in the political, as in the cultural sphere, in which Hinduism as a socio-religious system united the country in a way which was quite different from any political unity, and transcended its limitations".

One is tempted to say that the definitions of the Ancient Near East, of Central Eurasia and, to a lesser extent of China, are *per genus et differentiam*, whereas Islam and India can be defined by definite description. The reason for this is that "civilisation" and "barbarism" are corollary conceptions, whereas Islamic faith or Indian thought can be described without reference to any other religion or philosophy.

In the definitions given for each area the spiritual factors seem to have ascendance over the material in so far as identical language or economic conditions have apparently not the same amalgamating force as religion or a general consciousness of a superior civilisation. Such an impression is even strengthened by the observation that for three out of the five areas studied in this book, script is, if not a determining factor, at least the main vehicle of the spiritual content characteristic of them. The extension of Islam is the same as that of the Arabic script. The same applies to China. Pulleyblank rightly points out (p. 58) "that the nations [*mark the plural!*] which have adopted the Chinese script . . . however divergent they may be in some respect . . . can be called one family".

Economic factors, such as means of production, important as they may be, do not seem to determine the frontiers of the largest historical unities. Frankfort's statement is in this regard most significant (p. 6) : "we find in both countries [Egypt and Mesopotamia], even in prehistoric times, evidence of a well-balanced mixed economy in which agriculture and stock-breeding existed side by side and were supplemented by fishing, fowling and hunting". The unity of Islam includes nomads and cultivators, stock-raisers or merchants. Chinese economy is essentially based on agriculture but, although this may be a distinguishing feature when compared with Central Eurasia, it does not differentiate it from India. Two societies are here distinguished by their spiritual and not by their material content. The lines of solidarity run across and not parallel to the lines of occupation, although this only applies to those unities of the largest scale which are at present our sole concern.

All of the areas studied, with the exception of Central Eurasia, have, however, one common material constituent, which is economic. All are essentially sedentary, city-building societies, economically self-supporting and not bent on parasitism like Central Eurasia. The basic two-fold distinction of Asian humanity into civilised and uncivilised has its roots not in the spiritual, but in the material structure of the peoples concerned. The common constituent of the uncivilised is so powerful that no other characteristic is strong enough to form among them historical entities of long duration. The sedentary world on the contrary—less in China than elsewhere —is only partially aware of its basic unity and is then subdivided into unities of smaller scope in which the common constituents are of a spiritual rather than of a material order.

The main vehicle of this spiritual factor proves to be the script rather than the language. The foremost tool of human communication, the spoken word, does not seem to be essential to the creation of the greatest historical entities of Asia.

These somewhat abstract considerations may or may not be acceptable, but, in my view, they follow from what has been said by the authors. They are most certainly not based on preconceived ideas.

I was interested also to see all the authors stressing the importance of contacts between various civilisations and the emphasis laid, by at least four of us, on the economic factors of oriental history. This is surely a sign of present tendencies in historical writing.

As far as the study of oriental history is concerned, the picture drawn by the authors is far from being bright. Only for the Ancient Near East can the general historian rely—to quote Frankfort (p. 13)—"on an invaluable collection of up-to-date translations", and there is a fair amount of source-material on India which is available in translation. For the other areas, the amount and the quality of the material hitherto made accessible to the general historian seems utterly inadequate. Lewis' sentence, "The published sources are still only the visible tenth of the iceberg protruding above the surface of the waters, while the mass remains below, a danger to the unwary" (p. 17), can well apply also to other areas.

If the present rhythm of research remains unaltered it will need several generations to reach for Asia the same level of historical knowledge as we have at present of Europe. I am sure that all my fellow-authors, as myself, will feel satisfied if this booklet helps to advance one step further on the long road which lies ahead.

D. S.